Musical Intimacy

Musical Intimacy

Construction, Connection, and Engagement

Zack Stiegler and Todd Campbell

BLOOMSBURY ACADEMIC
NEW YORK • LONDON • OXFORD • NEW DELHI • SYDNEY

BLOOMSBURY ACADEMIC
Bloomsbury Publishing Inc
1385 Broadway, New York, NY 10018, USA
50 Bedford Square, London, WC1B 3DP, UK
29 Earlsfort Terrace, Dublin 2, Ireland

BLOOMSBURY, BLOOMSBURY ACADEMIC and the Diana logo
are trademarks of Bloomsbury Publishing Plc

First published in the United States of America 2023
This paperback edition published 2025

Copyright © Zack Stiegler and Todd Campbell, 2023

For legal purposes the Acknowledgments on pp. 138–139 constitute an extension of this copyright page.

Cover design by Louise Dugdale
Cover image: JGI/Jamie Grill/Getty Images

All rights reserved. No part of this publication may be reproduced or transmitted in any form or by any means, electronic or mechanical, including photocopying, recording, or any information storage or retrieval system, without prior permission in writing from the publishers.

Bloomsbury Publishing Inc does not have any control over, or responsibility for, any third-party websites referred to or in this book. All internet addresses given in this book were correct at the time of going to press. The author and publisher regret any inconvenience caused if addresses have changed or sites have ceased to exist, but can accept no responsibility for any such changes.

Whilst every effort has been made to locate copyright holders the publishers would be grateful to hear from any person(s) not here acknowledged.

A catalog record for this book is available from the Library of Congress.

ISBN: HB: 978-1-5013-7225-4
         PB: 978-1-5013-7229-2
         ePDF: 978-1-5013-7227-8
         eBook: 978-1-5013-7226-1

Typeset by Integra Software Services Pvt. Ltd.

To find out more about our authors and books visit www.bloomsbury.com and sign up for our newsletters.

Contents

List of Illustrations   vi

Introduction   1

Part I   Production

1   Conjuring Intimate Spaces   15
2   Intimacy and the Home Recording Aesthetic   29

Part II   Text

3   Textual Dimensions of Musical Intimacy   43
4   Analyzing Musical Intimacy   55

Part III   Additional Contexts

5   Marketing Musical Intimacy   89
6   Intimacy and Live Performance   105

Conclusion   131

Acknowledgments   138
Notes   140
References   143
Index   165

Illustrations

Figures

1	2 Over 3 Rhythm	61
2	"Ain't No Grave" Vocal Rhythm #1	74
3	"Ain't No Grave" Vocal Rhythm #2	75

Tables

1	The Structure of "Blue 7"	60

Introduction

Alison Fensterstock (2020) begins a 2020 piece on Las Vegas residencies by discussing Gwen Stefani's *Just a Girl* show, then slated for two final runs in a multi-year engagement at the Planet Hollywood Resort and Casino. In Fensterstock's assessment, "the truly arresting part of *Just a Girl* is the intimacy … and she [Stefani] leans into the intimacy of it." In concluding the piece, Fensterstock writes that "in Vegas, where the room is smaller and the bus isn't being packed up for a redeye drive and the artists at least appear to be a little more relaxed, the intimacy feels more real—between fans and fans, and fans and artists."

Since 2008, National Public Radio has produced its ongoing Tiny Desk Concerts, a streaming video series wherein musicians play abbreviated concerts in an office setting, promoted as "intimate video performances, recorded live at the desk of *All Songs Considered* host Bob Boilen" (National Public Radio n.d.). Assessing the series' first eight years, Zachary Crockett (2016) makes much of the "incredibly intimate, up-close, and personal" style of the videos, attributing this approach to the series' ongoing success.

The year 2018 saw the first posthumous release from Prince's storied vault of recordings—a solo piano rehearsal marketed as *Piano and a Microphone 1983*. In *Spin* magazine, Winston Cook-Wilson (2018) commented on the album's "near-voyeuristic intimacy." *The Guardian*'s Damien Morris (2018) discussed the album as "an intensely intimate experience," while Kory Grow's (2018) review in *Rolling Stone* described the album as "too unguarded and intimate even for an artist as bold as he was."

Bruce Springsteen's run of Broadway shows was similarly hailed as "an intimate spectacle" and "an intimate triumph" (Als 2017; Greene 2017). This rhetoric continued in the critical discourse surrounding the subsequent release of the show's associated Netflix special and accompanying soundtrack album. Writing about the album for Pitchfork, Caryn Rose (2018) provides a metatheoretical point, stating that "intimacy isn't simply a function of size and proximity; it's about connection, about vulnerability and the ability to effectively tell a story." In his review of the album for *Pop Matters*, Christopher John Stephens (2018) cautions readers that "the intimacy here can be overwhelming if the listener isn't careful."

The above writers highlight the persistence of a sense of intimacy across various musical contexts: live performance, streaming video, and sound recording. This suggests audiences' valuation of intimacy in popular music, and artists' work to cultivate such perceptions. But what does it mean for a deliberately constructed musical performance (live or recorded) to be "intimate?" Though the notion of intimacy is often employed in music criticism and the broader cultural discourse of popular music, scant attention is paid to what is meant by the term's common implementation. As Elizabeth Margulis (2019: 1) states of music more broadly, "we are generally not very good at talking about it," despite its pervasiveness in our everyday social, cultural, and personal lives.

As readers and fans, we have some understanding of what meaning the term might hold. However, this is at odds with the lack of a working definition of musical intimacy. This tension—between a seemingly shared understanding of intimacy in music and the dearth of discourse fully articulating it—is the impetus behind this book. Across contexts of performance, production, promotion, and recording, our analysis works to define and understand musical intimacy as both a concept and practice in popular music, as well as to understand the affective dynamics at play in musically intimate encounters.

Defining Musical Intimacy

Intimacy

The ensuing chapters will examine the notion of musical intimacy through a variety of contexts, examples, and analyses. In this Introduction, we build a foundational framework for moving forward. Before grappling with how we might define musical intimacy, however, we need to step back to address intimacy more broadly—noting that intimacy is itself a complicated, ever-evolving concept.

Cultural and social definitions of intimacy have shifted over time, as has the nature of intimate relationships (Gadlin 1977; Levenson 1974; Sexton and Sexton 1982). Tracing its etymology, Sexton and Sexton (1982: 1) note that in the term's Latin roots, "to be intimate with another is to have access to, and to comprehend, his/her innermost character." Typified by close interpersonal relationships, intimacy can take a variety of forms, including clinical, domestic, familial, and romantic, across emotional, informational, physical, and sexual dimensions (Beebe, Beebe, and Redmond 2010: 253; Froude 1876: 166–7; Karst 1980: 629; Urban Dictionary 2005; Zelizer 2007: 18). Across these conceptualizations, mutuality and relationality are at the core of intimacy. Correspondingly, mutuality and relationality establish an openness and intersubjectivity between parties, as through shared attention, knowledge, and trust unique to that particular relationship (Zelizer 2007: 17–18; see also Bersani and Phillips 2008; Bernhagen 2013; Oden 1974).

Our intimacy with others is not limited to directly interpersonal, face-to-face contexts, however. While intimacy may be characterized by an awareness and closeness between two parties, equally as essential is what transpires between them through communication, even if such exchanges are technologically mediated (Berlant 2000; Clinebell and Clinebell 1970; McClane 2000). Useful here is Hatfield's (1982: 271) argument that intimacy is not a static phenomenon, but an ongoing and fluid process. In other words, intimacy is not simply something that we encounter, but something with which we actively participate and engage.

Levinger and Raush (1977: vii) note the palpable tensions between our continued desire for closeness and intimacy and the increasing social distance from one another. As modern social, cultural, and economic forces encouraged such distancing, the rise of electronic mass media offered means for us to at least perceive the closeness and intimacy that were otherwise becoming difficult to achieve in our personal lives. An array of scholarship demonstrates such intimate encounters via telephone (Marvin 1990; Peters 1999), radio (Arnheim [1986]/1936; Douglas 2004; Hilmes 1997; Horton and Wohl 1956; Jarman 2013; Loviglio 2005; Scannell 1996), and digital platforms (Berryman and Kavka 2017; Burgess and Green 2018; Jerslev 2016; Johnston 2017; Lee and Watkins 2016; Sienkiewicz and Jaramillo 2019; Spinelli and Dann 2019). As this body of work suggests, neither physical distance nor technological mediation necessarily diminishes opportunities for intimacy formation and maintenance.

Musical Intimacy

Similar to broadcasting, telephony, and computer-mediated communication, popular music often lends itself a sense of intimacy simply by its means of delivery and consumption. Like broadcasting, we invite popular music into our domestic spheres and the privacy of our automobiles; similar to the telephone, earbuds physically rest within the outer ear, emitting sound waves to travel down our ear canals, and ours alone. Yet music is unique from these other examples in that it is not confined to a particular technological system. Music does not circulate solely in the fixed, point-to-point structure of the telephone nor the one-to-many dynamic of broadcasting. Certainly, music communicates through such structures, but it is also more ubiquitous and deploys across multiple platforms; for listeners, music is often not merely a matter of reception, but one of personal and social experience (Small 1998).

Musical meaning is not textually determined, but is significantly shaped by what Berger (2009: 5, 10–13) terms "structures of lived experience." Filtered through intersectional identity, our lived, everyday experiences (including education, geography, values, and belief systems, among other factors) influence how we make sense of the world, and help to account for divergent perceptions and meaning making among composers, artists, and audiences. This is important for our purposes in this book, as musical intimacy largely relies on matters of perception, and is not necessarily incumbent upon intentionality—although through a variety of musical and textual means, artists, performers, and composers certainly provide "indications of how to listen" (Frith 1996: 108–9). This is precisely what we mean by *constructions of musical intimacy* throughout the book: the ways that audience perceptions of intimacy might be primed in popular music recording, performance, and promotion. This emphasis on perception and meaning making at the individual level is not to disregard the social dimensions of music, including its role in collective identity, cultural meaning, and its reliance upon shared systems of meaning (Frith 1996: 269, 273; Kingsbury 1988: 110).

Musical intimacy is thus a unique kind of intimacy, though it belies a clear definition. There is surprisingly scant literature on the topic, although this body of work is growing, as scholars increasingly turn attention toward various aspects of music and intimate relations. More explicit notions of popular music and intimacy emerge in the body of scholarship studying vocal aesthetics in early broadcast and recording media, underscoring how the introduction of increasingly sensitive electric microphones led to the development of intimate vocal styles such as crooning (Lockhart 2003; McCracken 1999; McCracken 2015; Wijfes 2014). Musical intimacy also features in the literature on music therapy (e.g., Amir 1992; Arnold 1975; Edwards 2011; Borin and Dvorak 2018; Amir 1992; Andsell 2014; Austin 2002; Medcalf 2016a; Medcalf 2016b; Medcalf and McFerran 2016).

Scholarship that is more firmly situated in cultural studies, ethnomusicology, and related areas more explicitly addresses the relationship between music and intimacy in everyday life. Stokes (2010), for example, examines popular music as a locus of cultural intimacy, demonstrating how through its affectively charged lyrical content and sonic textures, popular music in Turkey both challenges and refigures dominant notions of Turkish identity. Drawing on Berlant's notion of intimate publics, Shank (2014: 16, 1–2) similarly argues that music is one force among many that brings the body politic into those shared social, cultural, and political relations modeled on "the experience of belonging to a community not of unity but of difference."

Other previous work considers how popular music can forge intimate interpersonal connections via shared musical experiences (e.g., Randolph forthcoming; Patterson 2019: 4; Bernhagen 2013). In her study, Bernhagen (2013: 22) defines musical intimacy as "a felt intersubjectivity brought about by musical experience when participants share an openness (resulting from a willingness to give oneself over, to be listening musically, and open to the momentary elusiveness of meaning) to that experience and to each other." Here, musical intimacy is centered on the ways that music creates and maintains interpersonal, social bonds among groups of listeners.

Cusick (2006: 74) similarly notes music's potential as an agent of interpersonal intimacy. However, she is especially concerned with encounters between solitary listeners and music itself. Cusick's thinking informs our own conceptualization and application of musical intimacy in this book. Rather than the facilitation of interpersonal connection, our examination of musical intimacy centers attention on understanding the positive relationality between music and listeners as a fundamentally unique, but woefully underexplored phenomenon. To that end, the book is driven by a series of broad questions. How does popular music conjure, engage, and exploit notions of intimacy? How is it that certain concert performances or recorded works—both highly constructed, mediated musical contexts—can be described and experienced as "intimate?" What are the musical affordances that give rise to such experiences?[1]

To offer answers to those questions, we build on this previous scholarship to define musical intimacy as *an affectively charged musical experience marked by a perceived sense of openness and relationality between artists, listeners, and texts*, or a variant combination thereof. Unlike physical, romantic, or sexual intimacy, musical intimacy does not necessarily require a mutual exchange; as in Horton and Wohl's (1956) theory of parasocial interaction, experiences of musical intimacy are often one-sided, with no direct personal interaction. Yet these one-sided experiences of musical intimacy should not be discounted as less meaningful or sincere, for as Hayes and Gravesen (2013: 145) argue, "audiences build real connections with media through the social networks that shape their reception of, and response to, media content."

It is also worth noting at the outset that we view the phenomenon of musical intimacy as engaging ideas of both inclusivity and exclusivity. Though seemingly contradictory, consider how music scenes can define boundaries between in groups (e.g., fans, artists) and out groups (everyone else). The duality of this dynamic operates to foster not only a sense of intimacy between listeners and artists, but within music communities, fandoms, and scenes (see, for example, Baym 2018; Beekhuyzen et al. 2011; Duffett 2017; Hagen 2010; Jarvenpaa and Lang 2011; McLeod 2001; Rapuano 2001; Verbuč 2017; Verbuč 2018). As we note in our discussion of reissues and archival recordings in Chapter 5, fans (as opposed to casual or disinterested listeners) have a greater affective investment in the artists of their fandom and, as a result, are likely to have a very different kind of engagement with musical intimacy than these other listener groups. This is simply to say that musical intimacy can be as much about exclusion as inclusion, and this is especially evident in the performance contexts that we examine in Chapter 6.

Throughout, this book approaches musical intimacy as a construction; in doing so, we do not suggest that listeners simplistically equate musical intimacy with interpersonal intimacy. Rather, the meaning and value that listeners ascribe to instances of musical intimacy are indicative of popular music's ability to facilitate a sense of connectivity between artists, texts, and listeners.

Music and Affect

Throughout the book, we approach these questions through a lens of affect theory, particularly the growing body of work on affect as a framework for understanding sound and music. As literature on affect theory has expanded in recent decades, one of its defining characteristics has been its lack of fixity (Figlerowicz 2012: 3; Seigeworth and Gregg 2009: 3, 9). This resistance to a strict, singular definition speaks to both the complex nature of affect as a construct, and its utility in understanding a broad array of relational dynamics. At its most basic, affect is sometimes defined in terms of emotion or mood, although these are in fact distinct entities (Thompson and Biddle 2013: 7–8). Like intimacy, however, affect is relational in nature (Thompson and Biddle 2013: 9), and can be thought of as "in-between-ness," the forces, intensities, and resonances "that circulate about, between, and sometimes stick to bodies and worlds, *and* in the very passages or variations between these intensities and resonances themselves" (Seigworth and Gregg 2009: 1–2, 13; emphasis in original). Shaviro (2012: 8) further clarifies this point, arguing that affect is not emotion or feeling per se, but "the particular *way* in which a given entity receives (prehends or perceives)" information or stimuli.

This "how" of affect is central to Teresa Brennan's (2004) work on the transmission of affect—the dynamics, properties, and effects of its circulation. Brennan's concern is primarily with the affective matrix of social interaction and physiological response. Even so, communication, technology, and art can also serve as media for the transmission of affect, be it unconscious or deliberately constructed—and this includes popular music (Thompson and Biddle 2013: 5).

Among the first to seriously consider popular music through the lens of affect theory, Lawrence Grossberg understands affect to be the primary means by which we experience and process popular music. Grossberg (1984: 226–8) considers the relationship between fans and popular music to be one of "affective investment," through which music "both locates and produces the sites at which pleasure is possible and important for its audiences; it provides the strategies through which the audience is empowered by and empowers the musical apparatus." Variably, the return on this investment covers a wide range of gratifications that music can engender, including empowerment, emotional stimulation, and a sense of *communitas* within a particular audience or fandom.

Marie Thompson and Ian Biddle (2013: 16) suggest that one way to approach the relationship between music and affect "is to think [about] sound and music as offering ways of *manifesting* affect ... facilitating acoustic entry into affective fields, as offering a way to both abstract and particularize affective states and as furnishing a reflective medium for imagining affect 'itself'" (emphasis in original). We adopt this framework in our study of musical intimacy. Through establishing the listener's subjectivity, popular music becomes more than a commodity or a text. While it is both of these things, popular music also serves as an entry point to access, channel, and manifest affect, allowing for intimacy to be effectively exploited and perceived. In other words, popular music serves as a structure through which intimacy and "in-betweenness" circulate between artist and audience.

The very nature of this structure is central to popular music's affective capacities. Popular music operates as what media scholar Paddy Scannell (2000: 9) terms a for-anyone-as-someone structure, one that "is always, at one and the same time, for me *and* for anyone ... The for-anyone-as-someone structure expresses 'we-ness.' It articulates human social and sociable life" (emphasis in original). Scannell applies this lens to discuss how through framing and modes of address, radio and television broadcasters are able to speak to audiences as individuals, despite being anonymous members of an amorphous, undefined mass. Scannell contends that such approaches are what lend a sense of believability and sustained credibility to broadcast personalities. This is in part what enhances popular music's affective capabilities as well. Although the means of production, distribution, and consumption evolve along with changes in technological trends, popular music is primarily a mass-produced and -distributed product that is inherently "for-anyone," regardless whether the music in question is accessed via a vinyl record, a live concert, an online audio stream, or the background music being piped into a public space.

Importantly, these technologies of distribution and consumption provide pathways not only for the circulation of popular music, but also for its associated affect, as music's "distributedness mimics, apes or models the affective field in its non-locality, by calling attention to the structures of affect, affection and affiliation that characterize the work of the sonic" (Thompson and Biddle 2013: 16). We argue that it is popular music's affective qualities that give rise to musical intimacy, in terms of how it is constructed, experienced, and perceived—despite the spatial, temporal, and experiential distance that typically exists between artist and audience; this is true across the various permutations of musical intimacy that we analyze in the following chapters of the book.

Outline of the Book

The remainder of this book is divided into three sections that each serve to better understand the aesthetic, relational, and sonic properties of popular music that yield perceptions of intimacy among listeners. Because recorded music remains the predominant way that we listen to and experience popular music, much of our attention is focused on the processes and products of such recordings. A primary factor in creating and perceiving musical intimacy concerns space. Part One centers on the recording process, and how sites of music production shape the sonics of recorded works, as well as how the recordings-as-texts evoke those spaces. Recordings of popular music work to capture and conjure a particular space, be it the recording studio, a performance venue, or the diegetic space of a lyrical narrative. In any case, technologies and strategies in engineering, production, and aesthetics work to construct imagined, intimate spaces that also provide unique opportunities for listeners to engage with recordings and the artists' personae.

With our focus on the aesthetics and sonics of popular music recordings, the studio plays a crucial role in our analysis. As sites of music production, recording studios are also where constructions of musical intimacy take shape. Particularly in relation to commercial recordings then, studios are also sites of power. The role of social identity is a concern throughout the book, but we pay it particularly close attention in Chapters 1 and 2. Noting the tendency of large format recording studios to be spaces dominated by white male identities (particularly in the roles of engineer and producer), we consider the marginalization of non-dominant identities within these spaces.

In contrast, the growth of home recording in recent decades offers opportunity for the potential empowerment of independent musicians, particularly those from marginalized groups. As such, home recording stands to have quite a different impact on the construction of musical intimacy and perceptions of authenticity, as it affords opportunity for greater artistic autonomy and self-representation. Thus, whereas Chapter 1 focuses on professional studio environments, Chapter 2 considers how the increasing affordability and accessibility of the home recording (or "prosumer") environment fosters musical intimacy on different terms, inherently constrained by limited rather than abundant resources. Here too, the recording context can generate musical intimacy via aesthetics and fidelity as well as building a perceived authenticity via artistic ethos. Through analyzing recordings by Daniel Johnston (1981), Elliot Smith (1995), Dévon Hendryx (2013), and Billie Eilish (2019), this chapter demonstrates the impact that the rise of home recording has had in establishing a unique source of musical intimacy.

Part Two shifts to explicitly focus on popular music recordings as texts, and how musical intimacy typically manifests within such recordings. To do so, in Chapter 3 we develop a four-dimensional analytic framework for examining intimacy in popular music recordings, including focus on voice, lyrics, song construction and form, and sonic spatiality. To explicate this framework, Chapter 4 applies it to a diverse quartet of recordings, including works by Sonny Rollins

(1956), Prince (1982), Johnny Cash (2010), and Fiona Apple (2020). Through analysis of these specific recordings, we uncover precisely how these dimensions can work in concert to establish a sense of musical intimacy with the listener.

Although much of this book considers popular music in its recorded forms, Part Three acknowledges that musical intimacy is not solely the purview of recorded work and pivots to two other areas to engage a deeper analysis. Given the deployment of "intimacy" in popular music discourse, it is apparent that musical intimacy has some sense of value for listener. This value is evident in the various ways that musical intimacy is continually marketed across a variety of platforms and products, and this is subject of Chapter 5. In particular, we consider the practice of mining studio vaults to package and release outtakes, worktapes, and home demo recordings that feature in the ongoing trend of archival releases and deluxe repackagings of classic albums. In the musical marketplace, such commodities trade on musical intimacy, suggesting the provision of sonic access to intimate, even private spaces, allowing listeners to sonically witness the intimacy of creative processes and performance. Chapter 5 considers how these sonic properties explicitly trade on notions of nostalgia and musical intimacy in how they are constructed and promoted in the popular music marketplace.

In Chapter 6, we turn to live performance to understand how musical intimacy can be conveyed from the stage. This is not merely a product of the close proxemics within a given performance space, though such spaces are a frequent subject in discourse surrounding intimate musical performances. To the contrary, a number of high-grossing, arena-filling acts are praised in critical and fan discourse for their ability to connect with live audiences, despite being but a single individual among 20,000 others. Taking the performance career of Bruce Springsteen as a case study, Chapter 6 examines this unique dynamic, and how performers are able to cultivate a sense of musical intimacy in defiance of the obstacles characteristic of such large-scale performance spectacles. Chapter 6 also brings an additional, unique performance situation under study that arose during process of writing this book. As the Covid-19 pandemic forced much of the world into social isolation in the spring of 2020, musicians quickly took to streaming platforms to broadcast informal performances, connecting their domestic spaces with those of their fans. This style of mediated performance quickly became normalized, as late-night talk shows and one-off musical events broadcast similar performances across primetime television and online platforms. This social and technological context provides opportunity to understand a unique kind of musical intimacy, manifested in mediated musical performance at a time when the need for a sense of connection and community was especially heightened. Finally, the Conclusion synthesizes the analyses and case studies of the preceding chapters, addressing broader questions about the persistence of intimacy in popular music, and centering on the complex relationship between musical intimacy and authenticity.

In 1934, John Dewey (1934: 237–8) ruminated on sound (and by extension, music) as inherently intimate, noting that "sounds *come* from outside the body, but sound itself is near, intimate; it is an excitation of the organism; we feel the clash of vibrations throughout our whole body" (emphasis in original). In her critical examination of Led Zeppelin more than six decades later, Susan Fast (2001: 131) makes a similar point in articulating that "sound touches us, physically. It connects us with the body from which it is coming. It is an intimate form of human contact. This may well be one reason that music is so powerful: it engages us physically and with the bodies of the musicians who are making it." Speaking in the context of legal definition and interpersonal intimacy, Karst (1980: 629) argues that "an intimate association … is more than the sum of its members, it is a new being, a collective individuality with a life of its own."

As an extension of Dewey, Fast, and Karst, we understand music as a phenomenon capable of a unique form of intimacy that, compounded by its affective dimensions, is a powerful component of popular culture. More than that, popular music's broad dissemination and social omnipresence create multivalent associations within the culture itself, between and among artists, texts, and audiences. In the chapters that follow, we work toward a greater understanding of these associations through the prism of intimacy and its various manifestations in popular music.

Part I

Production

1

Conjuring Intimate Spaces

Evolutions in technology have continually reshaped how engineers, musicians, producers, and audiences engage with popular music. Yet the primary means of popular music's circulation and consumption today is that of the recorded work, be it through radio broadcasting, physical media such as CDs and vinyl LPs, mp3 players, or, increasingly, audio streaming platforms. As a locus of production, the recording studio remains an important site in the popular music ecosystem, and is the central focus of the next two chapters. In the current chapter, we focus on large format, commercial recording studios and their output, while Chapter 2 shifts focus to the growing practice of home recording, which itself can take many forms. In both cases, we view the recording studio as a site where particular technologies and practices facilitate the construction of musical intimacy in the recorded work. Furthermore, both chapters are also concerned with how these physical spaces shape popular music recordings, and in turn, how such recordings reflect the relational dynamics and sonic characteristics of those spaces. While home recording setups and large format studios both engage with spatiality and intimacy, they do so in quite distinct ways. Through examining these contexts of music recording and production, these two chapters lay the foundation for our focus on popular music texts in the book's second section.

Marshall McLuhan's notion of acoustic space provides an early instance of conceptualizing the relationship between sound and spatiality though here, McLuhan is not especially concerned with sound media. Rather, Carpenter and McLuhan (1960: 67) outline spatial and relational characteristics of sound, pointing out that acoustic space has no fixed boundaries, is inherently dynamic, and is the "space made by the thing itself, not the space containing the thing." The acoustic space created by a New Orleans street busker, for example, extends as far as their sound can be heard. In this example, even nearby buildings are likely to reflect and diffuse the busker's music rather than dampen or contain it. If the same musician is brought into an acoustically treated studio, it is unlikely that the sounds they generate physically reach beyond the walls of the studio space, as such rooms are specifically designed to contain sound. Here then, the acoustic space is highly controlled and refined, extending relation only to those who may be present in the physical studio space.

McLuhan's broader concerns are the macro-level structures and relations that are shaped by communication technologies. These concerns are famously expressed in McLuhan's ([1962] 1967; see also McLuhan and Fiore 1968; McLuhan and Powers 1989) proclamation that the growing interconnectedness and collapse of distance brought about by broadcast networks facilitate a "global village," bringing geographically distant peoples into closer relation to one another, for good or ill. In regard to acoustic space, McLuhan's interest in broader media ecosystems invites us to consider not just the physical space defined by a particular sound, but also the intricate sonic networks established by the distribution of sound recording, and how this medium brings disparate spaces into relation with one another, regardless of the platform utilized. When a college student in 2023 streams Aretha Franklin's single "I Never Loved a Man (The Way I Love You)," doing so indirectly brings their dorm room into relation with Muscle Shoals' FAME studio, where Franklin cut the track in 1967 (even if this is not at the forefront of the student's mind while listening). This interconnected relationship of spaces grows ever more complex with the rise of digital platforms alongside deployment of broadband networks, as these developments afford opportunities for multi-site collaboration; individual parts can easily be recorded in geographically disparate locations, in addition to transformative processes of mixing and editing through pitch-correction, rhythmic correction, and other modern technologies. In short, the production, circulation, and consumption of sound recordings weave a complex web of spatial, aesthetic, and emotional relations that have bearing on the construction and ultimate perception of recordings' affective potential, including that of musical intimacy.

Recordings further evince their spatial origins through what Askerøi (2013: 17) describes as sonic markers, "musical codes that have been historically grounded through a specific context, and that, through their appropriation, serve a range of narrative purposes in recorded music." Askerøi's project takes up a variety of case studies to show how sonic markers are appropriated by and function within popular music. Most relevant to our concerns is a specific subcategory that he describes simply as "spatial markers," identifiable sonic markers of their cultural, geographic, and spatial sites of production. Such spatial markers are most evident when an identifiable scene or sonic branding develops around a core group of artists, producers, or studios. We can point to sonic palettes that became synonymous with particular cities and studios, including "the Motown sound" of the 1960s, Chicago House music in the 1980s, Bristol's trip-hop scene in the 1990s, or in Askerøi's study, how the music of Joy Division reflected the band's industrial hometown of Manchester.

The sonic representation of space plays a crucial role in the construction and perception of musical intimacy not only in terms of a recording's sonic properties, but through the relational connotations of such spatiality, that is, the physical relationships between people inhabiting and experiencing that sonic space. With these concerns in mind, our examination of the sites, spaces, and technics of popular music production in this chapter focuses on large format, commercial recording studios to answer questions of exactly how these spaces shape sound, and how the recordings that they produce sonically represent those spaces in ways that can bring listeners into a relational dynamic through the imagined network of sonic spaces described above.

The Role of the Studio Space in Enhancing Musical Intimacy

As studio technology evolved, pursuit of the optimal recording—at least according to the artist, producer, and label executives—was always paramount to the completed product. In the 1940s and 1950s, the recording engineer was not required to be concerned with aesthetics, and was instead focused on "the technical quality of the recording" (Schmidt Horning 2013: 24). However, as time progressed and technology matured in ways that accommodated increasing artistic demands, the recording studio became an expressive instrument as well (e.g., Eno [1979]/2017). This increasingly involved members of the recording and production team and both complementing and contributing heavily to the artistic and aesthetic visions in popular recorded music of the time.

The professional, large-format recording studio became the de facto environment for commercial popular music recording in the United States, particularly from the late 1940s to the end of the twentieth century. At the time, most studios that recorded and produced popular music were not always sonically pristine; many studios had a unique personality and sonic charm that was inviting and supportive of the artists and musicians who chose to work, create, and record there. Many studios had sonic idiosyncrasies that artists found appealing and desirable as a contribution to their artistic vision and aesthetic. To be sure, there were business considerations that factored into the decision to bring the actual recording process in-house and under the purview of the record label. However, the opportunity to create a controlled sonic environment built into the studio itself was enticing and often served to create and promote a label's signature sound—a compelling reason for the artist to record in their label's affiliated studios.

The intrinsic sonic fingerprint of the recording studio, coupled with a producer's vision that is competent, intentional, and focused, helped to enable artistic and aesthetic decisions that leveraged the role of the studio space itself as related to musical intimacy. When viewed longitudinally across myriad recording sessions, production teams, and commercial music releases, the producer of a recording session may well be viewed as a conduit through which the aesthetic decisions and direction of a studio session ultimately manifest through the music.

As an example, by the mid-1970s, the Record Plant in New York City was gaining a reputation for sonic experimentation on a commercially unprecedented level. Buoyed by record company largesse, the recording studios in the 1970s and 1980s were showered with massive recording budgets not seen before or since. The infusion of cash could often afford the luxury of sonic experimentation between and among the artists, the producers, and the rest of the production team. Campion (2015: 143) describes the Record Plant of this era as "an intimate space that expanded the range of sonic experimentation." Bob Ezrin, the producer for KISS's seminal 1976 release *Destroyer*, incorporated many sonic aspects of Studio A at Record Plant when recording the initial drum tracks, "moving the kit from one end of Studio A to the other ... into the deadened drum booth ... closer into the carpeted area ... and finally moving the bass drum and floor toms to the freight elevator for the monstrous backdrop to the cinematic themes of 'God of Thunder'" (Campion 2015: 161). Because of *Destroyer* and other records that were recorded, mixed, and produced there, The Record Plant as a creative force in the commercial music recording industry found itself at the epicenter of studios that were being actively sought out by producers and musical artists, in no small part because of how the studio's sonic idiosyncrasies contributed to the finished recording.

Recording studios have a characteristic sound, and it is up to the producer and engineer to exploit the studio's sound in ways that benefit the artist and the song. Discussing London's Abbey Road Studios 1 and 2 for example, Bennett (2016: 410) suggests that "the aura of the studio is transmitted in multiple ways: through the sound recordings made there; through artists and recordists who worked there," and "through the technologies that were used in the studio." Bennett's observation aligns well with the notion that the commercial studio's influence and impact on music recorded within was not transparent or sterile, and did not end simply with the recording console, the microphones, and other associated recording equipment. Rather, the studio provided a palpable history and a creative canvas—a site that already had a sonic texture and one that contributed to the recording process in ways that vitally enhanced the final product.

A recording studio's acoustic characteristics provide the basis for an embedded sonic texture that can contribute to and become a major determinant in the final recorded aesthetic. The idea of this sonic contribution is directly related to what Zagorski-Thomas refers to as functional staging of audio in a production, with the goal being to establish authenticity in order to enhance and promote musical intimacy. Zagorski-Thomas further argues that "the forms of spatial staging employed on recordings of singer/songwriters is another example of the way that function and audience aesthetic combine to produce normative practice" (Zagorski-Thomas 2010: 258). In essence, particularly through recordings released in the late 1960s through the turn of the century, common practice in the recording studio moved toward an acceptance of the studio itself as a principal and valued contributor to the artist's musical vision and resultant musical statement and aesthetic—even if there were events that some would consider to be anomalies, or worse, outright mistakes.

Inadvertent Intimacy

In addition to the rather conscious construction of musical intimacy in the studio, there are also instances of what we term "inadvertent intimacy." By inadvertent intimacy, we refer to extraneous sounds that are not part of the composition as such, but which nonetheless find their way into the recorded mix. Musical intimacy can be inadvertent as a result of unexpected sonic events that occur in a recording studio session or production environment. The acoustic, electroacoustic, or electronic sounds that studio engineers and producers perceive as inadvertent or accidental are often a result of production decisions made in consideration of the acoustic qualities of the studio, interactions between musicians and their instruments in the studio space, or a combination of both. Certainly, musical mistakes can be considered here, too. Bill Bruford (2019) considers a mistake to be "the unexpected outcome of unintended action … that provides evidence of human fragility, and hence intimacy. Musicians can be judged by their speed of reaction to unexpected outcomes; a wrong fingering, an unexpected feedback, a surprising sibilance in the room sound. These become part of the performance to the skilled practitioner." Such acoustic aberrations may seem like a distraction or mistake, but when heard in their proper sonic context, they can serve to reinforce constructions of musical intimacy to the listener, and become an inexorable, vital part of the fabric of the recorded piece. In assessing these sonic anomalies, we organize inadvertent intimacy into three common, but not mutually exclusive categories.

Instrumental Inconsistencies

Among the most common inadvertent intimacies in recorded popular music are instrumental inconsistencies—those unintended noises emanating from gear, furniture, or other non-musical objects within the recording space. Examples abound throughout the history of recorded popular music. In the acapella introduction of Kanye West's "Monster" (2010), a creaky studio chair is audible at 0:13–0:15, its presence underscored by the gaps of silence in between the song's layered, acapella vocal phrases. In another instance, the extended introduction Bruce Springsteen's "New York City Serenade" (1973) includes the especially noisy pedals of David Sancious' piano. At the 1:14 mark, the Miles Davis Sextet's recording of "Old Folks" (1961) bears an audible creak, the source of which is unidentified.

An especially notable subgrouping of instrumental inconsistencies is a persistently squeaky bass drum pedal audible in many popular recordings of the 1960s and 1970s. This distinct sound can be heard in the mix throughout the work of The Beatles, James Brown, Led Zeppelin, and The Meters, among others. One does not have to strain, for example, to hear this squeaking mechanism between the beats of Joseph "Zigaboo" Modeliste's bass drum in The Meters' "Cissy Strut" (1969), or that of John Bonham in Led Zeppelin's recording of "Since I've Been Loving You" (1970), the footwork of Jabo Starks on James Brown's "Super Bad" (1971), or "Big John" Thomassie's playing on "Heartattack and Vine" by Tom Waits (1981).[1]

The likely culprit in these recordings is the Ludwig Speed King pedal, an industry standard for decades (Ludwig 2001). Though it has roots in Ludwig's initial pedal manufactured in 1909, the Speed King first came to market in 1937 to wide adoption among drummers across genres. The Speed King was renowned for its smoothness, precision, and speed; due to its metal stirrup that connected the pedal to the cam assembly, it could also withstand heavy abuse. The Speed King's wide use in the latter half of the twentieth century accounts for the presence of its distinct squeak on recordings spanning decades, genres, and styles.

The noise itself is the result of the initial pedal's design and emanates from two sources. The first generates from the contact points of the link connecting the pedal plate and the rocker shaft assembly, especially when the lubricant on these moving parts begins to dry, increasing the friction between them. Squeaking can also occur when air leaks into the sealed joint compartments containing the pedal's ball bearings, drying out the lubricant on these joints as well (Mulholland 2012). In a concert setting, the squeak inherent in the pedal would be masked by the acoustic sound of the drums and the amplified instruments on stage. However, under the aural microscope of studio microphones, the pedal's extraneous noises often cut through the mix. Subsequent bass pedal designs by Ludwig and other manufacturers rectified this design flaw, though what colloquially became known as the "Squeak King" left its sonic imprint on popular music history.

Similar to the Speed King's inadvertent intimacy are musicians' seemingly unintentional, non-musical interactions with their instruments and gear. In the intro portion of Slipknot's "Duality" (2004), for example, the remnants of a metronome or click track can be heard beneath Corey Taylor's whispered vocals. Opening the Foo Fighters' debut album, "This Is a Call" (1995) is preceded by five seconds of intermittent electric noise, generated as Dave Grohl plugs his guitar cable into the guitar itself (the interference is resolved with a distinct click before Grohl begins the song proper). At the 3:45 mark in "White Moon" (2005), White Stripes drummer Meg White's bell setup collapses spontaneously, and remains in the final mix. A number of popular recordings also capture the distinct sounds of the drummer dropping their stick onto the studio floor, including Alice Cooper's "Be My Lover" (1971, at 3:01) and Julie Andrews recording of "Jingle Bells" (1966, at 1:40), while Aerosmith's "Sweet Emotion" (1975) captures the moment that the percussive vibraslap breaks (at 0:23).

Although such sonic occurrences are seemingly mistakes, their audibility in commercial recordings can convey a sense of transparency to listeners that further highlights the role of spatial markers, and works to place listeners into the sonic space of the studio. So strong are these connotations of transparency that in some cases, these sounds can now be added to a mix digitally, as in the case of "sympathetic snare buzz." This sonic event is common when musicians play together in the same space, and is most often provoked by the bass guitar's low frequencies resonating the wire snares of a bandmate's snare drum. AC/DC's 1976 recording of "Dirty Deeds Done Dirt Cheap" provides a clear example, most audible in the song's introduction (0:00–0:28). Likewise, "Body" by The Presidents of the United States of America (1995) bears sonic evidence of sympathetic snare buzz. However, the sound is typically imperceptible in commercial recordings either because individual parts are recorded in isolation, or the mixing balance masks the subtle, high-frequency sound. Yet "sympathetic snare buzz" is so indicative of co-spatial performance that software developer Wavesfactory (2021) offers a free audio plugin that allows producers to apply sympathetic snare buzz "as a psycho-acoustic effect to bring realism and life to your tracks"—yet another attempt at manufacturing a spatial marker of musical intimacy in the studio recording.

Corporeal Auralities

Inadvertent intimacies can also emanate from the people inhabiting studio spaces. This category of corporeal auralities encompasses intimate, non-musical, bodily sounds that get captured on recordings. While many of these sounds are orally sourced, they are not limited to vocalizations. For example, coughs are audible in the mix of "Wendy" by The Beach Boys (1964; 1:18–1:19),[2] "Foxy Lady" by the Jimi Hendrix Experience (1967; 1:03/1:06), Cornershop's "Brimful of Asha" (1997; 1:38), and "Walkie Talkie Man" by Steriogram (2004; 1:59–2:00).

Oral inhalations between vocal phrases are another common example of corporeal auralities. Because of the song's structure and mixing, these quick gasps for breath are especially pronounced in The Beatles' "Oh! Darling" (1969), where Paul McCartney makes use of a two-beat rest to draw breath before beginning each verse (as at 0:01, 0:34, and 1:40). Even in recordings with more sonic activity, pre-vocal inhalations are often audible as in the gaps between verse lines in Lizzo's "Juice" (2019; as at 0:20, 0:24, 0:28 for example), "Rainbow" by Kacey Musgraves (2018, as at 0:21. 0:25, 0:29, 0:38, 0:44, 0:52, 0:56. 1:00, 1:03), and Dua Lipa's "Swan Song" (2019, as at 0:20, 0:21, 0:23). Particularly in the Dua Lipa and Lizzo recordings, the breathy inhalations are somewhat subtle, a product of the overall sonic density of their mixes. This contrasts with The Beatles and Kacey Musgraves examples, the latter of which features close miking and a high mix/mic sensitivity, bringing such breathiness to the fore.

As with many of the inadvertent intimacies discussed in this chapter, digital mixing and editing have made it somewhat easier to mask these breaths if desired. Common practice and accepted production techniques of certain genres dictate that through either gating or digital editing, the inhalation of breath before vocal delivery should be deleted or minimized as much as possible. Yet when included in the track, their presence (however subtle) arguably adds to a perception of both intimacy and authenticity. This is perhaps why, like sympathetic snare buzz, post-production processing may be utilized to emphasize otherwise subtle sounds. Compressors in particular can be set to bring to quieter sounds on a vocal track (such as breaths) up to a level that is closer to that of the vocal performance proper. Such post-production treatment can underscore the unnatural balancing of these sounds. This is highlighted when occasional technological or editing errors that alter how these breaths come across in the recording can sound unnaturally jarring, as in Alanis Morissette's "Hand in My Pocket" (1995, at 0:22) and Janelle Monáe's "Crazy Classic Life" (2018, at 3:00).

Another subset of corporeal auralities are spontaneous vocalizations that are not necessarily part of the song's lyrics. During the percussive introduction to Toto's "Africa" (1982), a faint laugh is audible at 0:03. In Kamasi Washington's "The Invincible Youth" (2018), we hear someone yell "Yeah!" in the background at 7:13. In the Side B "Medley" of *The Black Saint and the Sinner Lady* (1963), a frustrated Charles Mingus exclaims "Godamnit!" at the 5:26 mark. Similarly, just before the first downbeat of Fleetwood Mac's "The Chain" (1977) someone can be heard whispering "Fuck!" to themselves. Underscoring the corporeality of the voice (or its grain, in Roland Barthes' terms), singer Merry Clayton's voice cracks at the 3:02 mark in The Rolling Stones version of "Gimme Shelter" (1969), which is followed by an excited "woo!" of encouragement from Mick Jagger in the background.

Whether they are audible as coughs, sniffs, gasps for breath, or profane exclamations, corporeal auralities puncture the notion of recorded popular music as unblemished, sonically ideal representations of musical performance. Instead, such sounds serve as reminders of artists' humanity, even within the controlled environment of a recording studio. Outside of the context of recorded media, these kinds of bodily sounds are only heard in close proximity to another person, in a shared physical space. Whether or not they are intentionally produced in the studio, corporeal auralities thus bring listeners into the sonic space of the recording studio, and also into intimate, sonic proximity with performers' bodies—a musical, sonic formation that mimics and evokes physical and spatial intimacy, which can in turn shape how listeners perceive and engage with musical texts.

Sonic Intrusions

Our third and final type of inadvertent intimacy is sonic intrusions, sounds that come not from musicians' bodies, equipment, or instruments, but from other objects within the acoustic space of recording. These include vehicular noise, as in Billie Holiday's 1935 recording of "Miss Brown to You," in which the sounds of traffic can be heard from beyond the studio walls at 0:31–0:32. Likewise in Led Zeppelin's "Black Country Woman" (1975); recorded outdoors at Stargroves in Hampshire England, the recording begins with the sound of an airplane passing overhead. An especially amusing, non-technological example of a sonic intrusion comes during the fadeout of "I'm Gonna Love You Too" (1958) by Buddy Holly, when we hear the chirping of a wayward cricket who had found its way into the studio's echo chamber (Amburn 1995: 80).

Communication technologies are also a common sonic intrusion in the studio, such as the ringing of a studio telephone in Ben Folds Five's "Steven's Last Night in Town" (1997, at 2:54), or the distinct sound of a digital watch alarm at a particularly hushed moment in The Flaming Lips' "What Is the Light?" (1999, at 0:55–0:56). Notably, this type of intrusion has evolved alongside contemporaneous technology, as in the sound of Facebook's Messenger interface in The Deftones' "You've Seen the Butcher" (2010, at 0:43) or the cell phone notifications at 1:19 in Tomemitsu's "In Dreams" (2016).

There are certainly examples that overlap between these three categories of inadvertent intimacies, especially between instrumental inconsistencies and corporeal auralities. This could be a horn player's draining their spit valve on Ella Fitzgerald's 1960 recording of "Have Yourself a Merry Little Christmas" (at 1:26), Lynn Easton's misguided drum stroke (and subsequent exclamation of "Fuck!") on The Kingsmen's 1963 version of "Louie Louie" (0:54–0:55) (Marsh 2004: 97), or Sting mistakenly sitting on a piano's keyboard, instigating the brief laughter at the beginning of "Roxanne" by The Police (1978) (Garbarini 2000).

Across these categories and combinations, what we've termed inadvertent intimacies potentially grant recordings a spontaneous, transparent, and intimate character, and thus forge a uniquely affective nexus of listener, performer, and the recording space. This is likely why some recordings are seemingly more intentional in their use of spatial markers. Walter "Wolfman" Washington's *My Future Is My Past* album (2018) begins with the sound of ice rattling in a glass, followed by Washington speaking into the mic, "Feel it." He takes a sip, then lets out an affirmative "mmhm." We then hear Washington set the glass down, say "Let's go to work," and slide his fingers across the fretboard before playing the opening chords of "Lost Mind." These are not background sounds but are clearly miked and/or mixed at unusually high levels to ensure that they are foregrounded. Given its placement preceding any of the album's music, and its technological treatment, this sonic gesture to intimacy is likely a conscious construction rather than inadvertent. This would be logical in the context of the album, conceived as being a "downtempo, really spacious, intimate" work, in contrast to Washington's previous recordings with his electric blues band The Roadmasters ('Ben Ellman', 2018).

The Walter "Wolfman" Washington example strongly suggests intentionality; yet when it comes to inadvertent intimacies in recordings of popular music, there is always some degree of intentionality, given the decision to retain such sounds instead of mixing them out, deleting them, or re-recording the take. Certainly, some of this may be attributed to technological constraints. For example, given the technological limitations of precision audio monitoring and the higher noise floor of analog tape, certain sonic anomalies like bass drum pedal squeaks may have gone unnoticed in the recording sessions of the 1970s and 1980s. With advanced noise reduction and equalization techniques applied to remastered versions of previously released material from that time period, original sonic aberrations are likely more audible than they were at the time of the original release. Likewise, when analog tape served as the primary recording medium, getting "the take" was a matter of capturing the musicians recording in the moment. If the overall feel of the take eclipsed other attempts, extraneous sounds were often accepted as the cost of using the desired take, and avoiding the process of recording yet another.

Although not "performed," these inadvertent intimacies become part of the recorded performance, and these extraneous sounds become "part of what is communicated" and "lend the recording an aura of transparency on a 'real' event" (Gracyk 1996: 79; see also Ake 2010: 39). A squeaky drum pedal or an off-mic sniffle may be an inadvertent, extramusical sonic incident, but when retained in commercial recordings, they effectively become part of the recorded text, and can thus serve as part of its appeal, as well as bearing individual meaning for listeners.

Gracyk (1996:56) further notes that the ability to hone in on such sounds is unique to recorded work, whereas they would receive little attention in the context of performance. But it is this very quality—extraneous sounds simply being part of the spatial environment, the acoustic space—that also grants them a quality of intimacy. Just as the microphone allowed for the hushed, intimate vocal style of crooning, technologies of music production and consumption afford listeners the possibilities of musical intimacy, to hear subtle inconsistencies both human and material from within the studio space, to draw listeners "inside the performer's instrument or respiratory system" (Ratliff 2016: 63). Our auditory system affords us selective hearing, and on repeated listening, we have the luxury of focusing on different aspects of the recorded performance. The ability to selectively focus on such spatial markers grants listeners sonic access to the studio space, wherein the sense of intimacy and transparency (regardless of intentionality) positions the listener as a kind of sonic witness, bestowing a sense of demystifying the recording process.

The Studio as a Site of Power

Jacques Attali ([1985]/2003: 87) reminds us that "possessing the means of recording allows one to monitor noises, to maintain them, and to control their repetition within a determined code … it allows one to impose one's own noise and to silence others." Put simply, recording studios are sites of power. This power is engaged in a number of ways; relevant to our concerns in this book, the decision-making of artists, engineers, and producers can guide and exploit listeners' perceptions of intimacy (Pinch and Bijsterveld 2004; Theberge 1997). This deserves examination when considering the dynamics of identities involved, and is perhaps most apparent when considering gender.

For example, in its analysis of *Billboard*'s Hot 100 Year-End Charts, a USC Annenberg study found that women accounted for approximately 2 percent of all production credits in 2020, while "no woman of color was credited as a producer on a song released in 2020 that made the Hot 100 Year-End Chart in the same year" (Smith et al. 2021: 15–16).³ The commercial recording studio thus remains a highly gendered space, and the role of the producer remains male dominated. This raises a host of important issues in considering how gendered power dynamics play into the production of popular music, and of musical intimacy. Reddington (2018: 60) outlines the phenomenon of gendered ventriloquism in popular music production, as when male producers mediate female artists (and their particular presentation of femininity), while Wolfe (2020: 186) argues that male producers also stand to control how female artists express emotion in their recordings. Reddington (2018: 62) points to the recordings of 1960s girl groups as particular example of this phenomenon, as they often relied on male songwriters and producers to craft the emotional perspective of teenage girls.

We can similarly extend Wolfe's point to account for the complex dynamics of how producers control the construction of musical intimacy in popular music. And while gender may be the most glaring example, producer-artist dynamics along axes of age, race, and sexuality can establish similar power differentials that stand to privilege a producer's conception of effective or meaningful sonic constructions of intimacy and emotion over those of the artist. The listener figures into this dynamic as well, for if some configuration of producers, engineers, and artists aim to construct a sonic sense of intimacy in their recording, they do so by anticipating what sonics are most likely to be perceived as such by the listener. This is not to suggest that these constructions are always effective of course, nor that the power and privilege producers can wield over artists and listeners are necessarily malevolent, but that these dynamics can have direct bearing on approaches to recording in general, and the particular constructions of musical intimacy in a given recording. For example, a middle-aged, white male production team recording a young Black female vocalist will likely shape the vocalist's sonic identity in ways that may not be consonant with her own artistic vision, identity, or intent—precisely the kind of ventriloquism Reddington (2018) highlights.

However, shifts in the industry, production, and practice of popular music suggest that while large format studios remain sites of power, artists' reliance upon them has diminished with the advent and increasing affordability and popularity of prosumer hardware and software for home recording. This is further underscored with the minimal barriers-of-entry to digital distribution platforms, through services such as Bandcamp, DatPiff, SoundCloud, DistroKid,

CDBaby, and others. Home recording and digital distribution offer artists a means to circumvent the established music industry-as-gatekeeper's stranglehold on distribution structures in ways that were simply not possible in earlier eras. In contrast to the power dynamics of commercial studios then, home recording and DIY distribution workflows present opportunities for artists to reclaim and retain some of that power; they also offer a decidedly different dimension to the construction of musical intimacy, and this is the focus of Chapter 2.

2

Intimacy and the Home Recording Aesthetic

Toward the end of the twentieth century, home recording gradually emerged as an affordable and accessible option for music production. Concurrently, advances in the digital infrastructure of the internet afforded alternative means for music distribution and consumption. Taken together, these developments have helped to shift the power dynamics of the popular music industry, reducing barriers of entry and affording greater access and control to artists. In addition to these macro-level benefits, home recording creates unique opportunities for the facilitation of musical intimacy. Framed within the DIY ethos of the domestic setting, home recording often lacks the controlled sonic environment of a professional studio in favor of a uniquely creative and intimate space. In addition to being highly personal, home recording can provide a sense of freedom and comfort to the artist that could be stymied in a professional environment where studio time comes with a hefty price tag (Watson, Hoyler, and Mager 2009).

In practice, the context and technique of home recording can vary widely. At a base level, home recording is a creative musical practice wherein most or all of the recording and subsequent production of a musical work occur in a domestic space. Since the late 1970s, home recording equipment has become more accessible and affordable for consumers. Currently, home recording hardware and software are capable of approaching the sonic caliber of large-format studio productions. Of course, the user's experience and adeptness with the intricacies of recording and production impact the final result, no matter the quality of the equipment being used.

The evolution of home recording can be framed in terms of affordances: what a particular entity offers, provides, or furnishes the individual (Gibson 1979: 127). Discussing technological affordances, Graver (1991: 79–80) suggests that the concept is not simply about the device or process itself, but also about the user, and the interactions between the two. Home recording brings with it multiple layers of affordances for artists, both economic and technologically based, and these are inextricably linked. The next section provides some context for the emergence of these affordances, as well as distinguishing home recording from large format studio practices.

A Brief History of Home Recording

A significant first step came with the introduction of the Ampex Model 200 in 1948. The recording industry was immediately transformed by the technological and creative possibilities of recording to tape as opposed to real-time disc recording, but the initial cost was prohibitive to most consumers, retailing for US$5,000 (US$60,642 in 2022 dollars) (Ampex 200A). Consumer-level reel-to-reel machines soon followed, and in 1962, the compact audio cassette came to market. These more affordable (albeit technologically limited) options allowed artists to craft demonstration tapes to be used as reference material in the process of making a proper studio recording.

By the mid-1960s, some established musicians began to acquire recording hardware for installation in a home studio environment. Pete Townshend (1983) was an early proponent of home recording, later proclaiming that "home recording produces moods and music, innocence and naivety that could be arrived at in no other way. Music that was never intended to be heard by a wide audience; notes and scribblings take on a new value assembled in this way." Yet Townshend operated from a position of substantial privilege, with home recording still requiring significant resources and capital. Not only was home recording equipment still expensive at this early stage, but it was also cumbersome and required detailed maintenance for optimum performance—resources that were not within reach for most consumers.

In 1979, Tascam introduced the Portastudio 144, a small, four-track recorder/mixer combo that recorded to standard cassette tapes ("TEAC—The History of Sound and Recording," 2022). With an initial retail tag of $899, the Portastudio 144 was still costly, but much more accessible than the $5,000 Ampex Model 200. The introduction of MIDI in 1983 was another watershed moment, as it dramatically increased the possibilities of instrumentation available to the home recordist. Multi-timbral MIDI keyboards, digital samplers, and ROMplers[1] allowed the home studio to emulate a wide variety of prerecorded instruments at the user's whim. MIDI's approximation of these instruments was not a perfect replacement for the real thing, but often the convenience, time, and money saved far outweighed the sonic deficiencies.

By the early 2000s, the growth of the home computer market alongside increasingly powerful microprocessors allowed home recording to take another major step forward. With personal computers capable of processing and storing large amounts of data, recording, mixing, and editing audio at home became possible. At the same time, digital recording was budget-friendly, ranging from modular DAW (Digital Audio Workstation) controllers and high sample-rate audio interfaces to extended range MIDI-capable effects processors and digitally programmable patchbays. Recording software such as Adobe Audition and ProTools grew increasingly sophisticated, while simpler, user-friendly programs such as Audacity and Garageband made digital recording even more widely accessible. The increasing affordability of such hardware and software made the practice of home recording realistically attainable for the consumer market, dispensing with costly studio time, product manufacture, and retail distribution costs inherent in the mainstream commercial music industry. In addition, home recordists now have access to specialized knowledge related to recording processes and techniques through a growing body of online resources.

The growth of home recording of course did not completely democratize music recording. Some research suggests that home studios have simply replicated the white male dominance of professional studios (Bell 2015). Still, the digital era of home recording undeniably lowered barriers to entry, and alongside the affordances of independent, online distribution, shook up the traditional dynamics of the popular music industry. As equipment available to the home recordist started to rival that of the professional studio, home recordists were able to experiment, explore, or pursue other musical ideas, and hone their craft without the time and budgetary pressures associated with an external, professional studio (De Carvalho 2012: 2).

From early tape recording through today's digital audio workstations, home recording has presented a variety of opportunities for musical intimacy, be they a product of acoustics in the domestic space or the limitations of home recording technology. We argue that the home recording environment produces distinct forms of musical intimacy through the home recording aesthetic, which we explicate below.

The Home Recording Aesthetic

As discussed in Chapter 1, the site of recording activity necessarily shapes the recording itself, or as Goold and Graham (2019: 133) put it, "the recording space is not incidental to recording." The sonic qualities of a given space are a genuine part of the finished recording, and this can be more readily apparent in home recording environments as opposed to large format commercial studios. The particular sonic, spatial, and environmental characteristics of the domestic recording space also lend themselves to distinct forms of musical intimacy, a result of what we describe as the *home recording aesthetic.*

By the home recording aesthetic, we refer to how such recordings bear the unique sonic characteristics of the home recording environment, including those that large-format recording studios often work to avoid. This aesthetic is a direct result not only of the recording space, but also of the artists' hardware and software choices, as well as the limitations of those choices. Notably, the quality of home recordings continues to increase as software becomes more sophisticated, equipment is increasingly tailored for the home environment, and recordists have access to an ever-growing body of knowledge through various digital resources. As equipment and software improve, home recordings come ever closer to replicating the quality of professional studio productions. Even so, many contemporary recordings continue to exemplify home recording aesthetics, with all that might be described as the unique charms, limitations, and idiosyncrasies of the home recording space; recordings by Hayley Williams (2021), Fiona Apple (2020), Prince (2001, 2018), and Bon Iver (2007) are just a few recent examples. In the more detailed discussion that follows, we perform a close analysis of home recording aesthetics across an admittedly purposive sample of four recordings. These recordings—by Daniel Johnston, Elliott Smith, Dévon Hendryx, and Billie Eilish—span four decades, and thus work within the technological affordances and limitations of each. The diversity of this small sample emphasizes that the home recording aesthetic is not solely a product of analog home recordings, nor of particular genres. Each of these recordings demonstrates home recording aesthetics in very different ways; yet, all promote musical intimacy as a result.

Daniel Johnston "Grievances"

"Grievances" comes from Daniel Johnston's first collection of recordings, *Songs of Pain*. Initially distributed to friends and peers while Johnston was still in high school, the collection saw wider release in 1988 on the independent Stress

Records label. The album takes on a decidedly lo-fi aesthetic that underscores the limitations of the simple cassette recorder that Johnston used to record it. Recorded in the basement of his parents' home, there is no obvious consideration of studio treatment, added effects, or any additional production. The nakedness of the production overall provides an unfiltered perspective into the raw emotional charge of the song's lyrical content. Writing for the *Austin Chronicle*, Ken Lieck (1999) described the song as "whipping effortlessly between wistful, cheery pop and somber, longing ballads," and introducing "themes and characters that remain integral to Johnston's oeuvre, most notably that of his boundless love/obsession with a young lady the singer believed he was fated to marry." At a basic level, "Grievances" exudes musical intimacy because of its utter lack of pretense.

The instrumentation on "Grievances" is simple but effective, consisting only of upright piano and vocal. The recording begins with Johnston clearing his throat and blowing into the cassette recorder's internal microphone, sounds that could have been easily edited out—even on Johnston's rudimentary setup. Yet these sounds serve an important purpose for musical intimacy, in that they allow the listener to be with the performer immediately prior to the start of the song, establishing an intimate sonic framework. In a way, we know what is coming before we hear the actual music, as we are being subtly acclimated to Johnston's voice and the noisy, distorted sonic character of the actual recording. It only takes a few seconds of hearing the tape hiss and background noise to give the listener an accurate sense of space, and moreover, a clear sense of the overall recording aesthetic.

The recording bears the aural signifiers of both its age and the extremely limited resources of Johnston's recording setup at the time, which consisted of a standard $59 Sanyo cassette recorder and Radio Shack cassettes; no additional microphones, no mixer, no processing equipment or software (Yazdani and Goede 2007: 7). As a result, the home recording aesthetic of "Grievances" is decidedly lo-fi, rich with tape hiss and background noise, and has an overall amateurish quality that fans understand as part of its charm, while other listeners may find it annoying, unprofessional, or even unlistenable. Yet the poor, amateurish quality of the recording helps to give both a sense of the space and context of recording: a nineteen- to twenty-year-old using limited available resources to create music in his parents' basement in the pre-digital era (Yazdani and Goede 2007: 7).

"Grievances" could easily be construed as a demo recording, rife with what some might perceive as sonic and technical shortcomings: constant tape hiss, an imperfectly tuned piano, ambient noise, an unsteady tempo, and the subtly wavering intonation of the lead vocal are far from the markers of a professional recording. Yet it is precisely these elements that give rise to musical intimacy in "Grievances," bringing listeners a particular space and time, to hear Johnston's naked expression of unrequited love.

Elliott Smith "Needle in the Hay"

Released in 1995, "Needle in the Hay" is the opening track from Elliot Smith's self-titled sophomore album. Reviewing the album for its twenty-fifth anniversary, Sam Sodomsky (2020) remarked on the powerful yet sparse arrangements that characterized the record. To that end, the instrumentation for "Needle in the Hay" consists only of acoustic guitar and the lead vocal; however, the guitar track is doubled by an overdubbed second acoustic guitar, and the vocal is also duplicated via overdubbing in the song's choruses. Doubling tracks is a traditional approach in the studio when trying to thicken a sound, dating back to the early days of multitrack recording. Although the instrumentation in "Needle in the Hay" is sparse, this doubling provides a more rounded and layered overall sound, while maintaining an uncluttered mix that foregrounds Smith's solo performance.

As a product of home recording, the sonic ambience of "Needle in the Hay" is very small, almost non-existent, as is its apparent production. However, it is precisely this sparse ambience and stripped-down production aesthetic that promotes musical intimacy. In the context of audio production, sonic ambience is often correlated with reverberation, understood to be the persistence of a sound after its final decay (Moylan 2012). In general, longer reverberation times push a sound source further back in the mix, distant from the listener's point of audition. Conversely, shorter reverberation times, due to similar psychoacoustic cues, place a sound source in closer proximity to the listener. The almost complete absence of reverberation in "Needle in the Hay" moves the source even closer to the listener, resulting in a musically intimate transaction that further gains impact through the lyrical content and sparse arrangement, particularly as the piece alternates from the verse to chorus throughout the song's progression.

Journalist Jade Gomez (2020) points out that Smith's "compressed, almost claustrophobic" original recording of "Needle in the Hay" "sounds like it was recorded in an empty bedroom. In the remastered version, you're *in* that bedroom. The already uncomfortable intimacy is heightened by enhanced vocals that feel almost voyeuristic."[2] This intimate sense of sonic space is further enhanced by Smith's lyrics, which detail a sense of self-doubt, emotional torment, and by some interpretations, turning to heroin as a means of escaping these struggles. Such personal and emotionally charged lyrics dovetail with the sonic intimacy of space to craft a home recording aesthetic that lends a confessional quality to track.

These elements of intimacy are supported musically and lyrically on several levels, all of which contribute to the broader sense of musical intimacy conveyed by the track. For example, the incessant eighth-note rhythm played by the acoustic guitar does not fit easily into a four-beat measure. The syncopation and ambiguous nature of the time signature underscore the lead vocal in a particularly unsettling fashion, because it is not what we would logically expect in a standard musical context. Usually, we assume the musical accompaniment will support or complement the main vocal delivery. In the case of "Needle in the Hay," the accompanying guitar and imprecise time signature provide a jarring contrast to the vocal performance, drawing even more attention to the vocal delivery. While these individual musical and production elements convey musical intimacy on their own, they work in concert for an overall aesthetic of intimacy, underscored by the knowledge that recording took place at drummer Tony Lash's home.

Dévon Hendryx, "Ballad of a Poor Man"

Dévon Hendryx was an early stage name of Barrington DeVaughn Hendricks, a rapper who began gaining notoriety through mixtapes in 2009, and now records as JPEGMAFIA. Released in 2013, *The Ghost~Pop Tape* is the sixth release from Hendryx, recorded while stationed in Japan with the United States Air Force. Hendryx has openly discussed this as an emotionally fraught time in his life, including a 2020 tweet where he stated, "I won't lie … some of my old shit is hard to hear now … especially the ghost pop tape [sic]. I was very close to death when I made this" (JPEGMAFIA 2020). *Ghost~Pop*'s opening track "Ballad of a Poor Man" puts this depressive emotional state on full display, with a musical backdrop that reflects both the intimacy of Hendryx's recording space and the frank vulnerability of the song's lyrics, all packaged in a production style that presents a unique home recording aesthetic.

Ghost~Pop's liner notes simply state that the song was "recorded in the bathroom."[3] Supporting this, as the track begins, we hear water sounds, sniffles, phone notifications, whistling, percussive noises (including what could be interpreted as the cocking of a pistol at 0:39–0:42), and other ambient noise marked by the familiar reverberation of a bathroom, an inherently intimate space. It is a full twenty-seven seconds before we hear sustained passage of music, providing ample time for listeners to immerse themselves in the sonic ambience of the track.

A fully solo recording, "Ballad of a Poor Man," features Hendryx on vocals, guitar, piano, and bass, along with programmed drumbeats. The electronic instruments (bass, drums, and synthesized piano) have a noticeably different timbre, lacking the natural reverberation of the bathroom. Although the liner notes do not confirm this, it is likely that these electronic instruments were recorded to the Digital Audio Workstation either directly or via preprogrammed plug-ins. In either case, the bass, drums, and piano do not interact with the physical space in which Hendryx chose to record the vocal and guitar tracks. While these instruments provide a complementary texture to the live tracks, they do so in a way that supports the haunting reverberations of the vocals and ambient noise. Hendryx plays the piano harmony in soft triplets, enveloped in a secondary synth line that provides a sustained ethereal backdrop throughout. The bass subtly propels the movement of both the synth and keyboard lines; during the verses, the drums are similarly subdued, with only the isolated kick drum accenting the root bass notes. Amid this muted, dreamlike backdrop, the snare forcefully cuts through to signal the chorus before disappearing again, resubmerging into the track's murky soundscape.

Like the snare drum, the underlying bed of ambient noise also drops out of the mix completely during each verse (at 1:07–1:17; 1:28–1:38; 1:47–1:57; 2:07–2:17; 2:28–2:38; and 2:49–end/3:14). The absence of both the snare drum and the ambient noise creates a sonic shift in the recording that effectively places emphasis on the vocal performance in the verse, where Hendryx's lyrics have their most intense expressions of depression, hopelessness, and suicidal ideation. In the second verse for example, Hendryx admits that he wants to commit suicide, but lacks the courage to do so. In the penultimate verse however, he declares, "But my face gon' meet this gun."

The musical intimacy of "Ballad of a Poor Man" would be difficult to approximate in the sonically controlled environment of a professional studio. The combination of the song's instrumentation, production style, and sonic spatiality crafts a home recording aesthetic that mirrors the dark isolation expressed in Hendryx's lyrics. The song is jarring in its frankness about depression, loneliness, and suicide, an intimate emotional state further enhanced by the recording's reverberant bathroom acoustics, muted production style, and jarring snare hits, culminating in a compelling example of how a home recording aesthetic can facilitate musical intimacy.

Billie Eilish "All The Good Girls Go To Hell"

Billie Eilish is a vibrant example of an artist for whom home recording and independent distribution presented opportunities that may not have been accessible through the mainstream music industry. Eilish recorded her full-length 2019 debut *When We All Fall Asleep Where Do We Go?* in her parents' home, affording a greater sense of comfort and creative energy. This general ambience is captured in the song's outro, where we hear a casual, playful interaction between Eilish and her brother/creative collaborator Finneas O'Connell. Discussing the pair's decision to record at home, O'Connell cites the sterility and cost of commercial studios as deterrents, stating that large format studios "tend to be lifeless and without any natural light, so I wanted to record wherever we lived. We just don't want to be bound to a studio to who we'd have to pay untold sums to" (Daly 2019). As a product of home recording, *When We All Fall Asleep …* demonstrates a home recording aesthetic that values timbral shifts to generate contrast and enhance the musically intimate exchange between the artist, song, and the listener. From a compositional and production standpoint, critics praised the album for its creative risks and unorthodox production (e.g., Smith 2019; Snapes 2019; "Billie Eilish is" 2019). "All the Good Girls Go to Hell" is exemplary of the album's overall aesthetic approach.

The production values of "All the Good Girls Go to Hell" embody the polished, yet DIY aesthetic that frames the entire album. Home recording artists as well as commercial engineers often anticipate what kinds of equipment consumers are likely to use to listen to the released recording, optimizing the mix for that particular mode of listening. Irish producer Garret "Jacknife" Lee relayed this in discussing the album's production, noting that in relation to intimacy, Eilish and Finneas "recognized the power of the personal experience, maybe because everyone is listening on personal headphones. Small sounds are impactful. There are lots of new ideas. Those are the anomalies I'm talking about" (Crane 2022: 38).

As with the album as a whole, the instrumentation on "All the Good Girls Go to Hell" is overwhelmingly electronic, with few (if any) acoustic instruments audible in the mix, save for the vocals; and it is Eilish's vocals that most clearly influence the musical intimacy of the recording. "All the Good Girls Go to

Hell" features multiple vocal tracks by Eilish, recorded in very close proximity, meaning the microphone is quite close to the singer. It is clearly audible that Eilish sings each vocal track at a subdued, quiet, almost melancholic dynamic level. Proximity effect, or the low-level boost associated with closeness to a directional microphone, is also evident throughout the track, and Eilish leverages this psycho-acoustic phenomenon to further enhance the intimate quality of the lead vocal. This proximity effect in the recording process yields a similar result in listening to the recorded track; Eilish's voice sounds noticeably "close" to the listener, an effect that is heightened by listening through personal headphones, underscoring the aforementioned comment by Lee regarding listening technologies.

More specifically, the lead vocal track is unmistakably prominent in the mix. But here, we are confronted with the contrast of the vocal's timbre in opposition to where it is placed in the mix. Eilish's vocal is little more than a whisper throughout the track. When we hear a whisper, we associate it with proximity and intimacy, for we would not be able to hear such a hushed voice at a distance; these elements cause us to lean in, to actively concentrate on what is being said. The lead vocal on this track, however, is not placed according to where its timbre would suggest in a natural recording environment. Rather, it is more prominent than most other instruments in the mix. It is precisely this juxtaposition—a timbre associated with a quiet, in-your-ear, intimate sound but placed in a different dynamic context—that gives rise to musical intimacy within this particular recording. Notably, O'Connell and Eilish recorded vocals with an Audio-Technica AT2020—a large diaphragm condenser microphone that retails for under $100. With inherent self-noise and frequency response typical of an inexpensive microphone, the choice of the AT2020 contributes an undeniable quality to the production (Harvey 2022). Such an effect could arguably be achieved in professional studio setup. But the combination of consumer-grade equipment, freedom to experiment, and the domestic recording environment collectively shapes the recording and the musical intimacy it embodies.

Conclusion

The rise of the home recording studio has been greatly accelerated by technological innovation. In contrast to its earliest incarnations, home recording is now normalized thanks to increasingly affordable hardware and software options available to the home recordist, alongside the growing ease of digital distribution and promotion. This has undoubtedly provided artists an enhanced platform compared to the predigital era, and this has been especially important in decentering the commercial studio as a site of power. The affordances of home recording stand to destabilize the dominance of commercial recording studios, with potential implications for greater diversity and representation of marginalized groups.

This is not to say that commercial studios have become obsolete, nor that they have abandoned their gatekeeping function or their maintenance of status quo power dynamics. But it does mean that a bipolar introvert, a budding solo musician, a discharged Black Airforce vet, and pair of teenage siblings can record their work, navigate alternative distribution channels, and achieve varying degrees of commercial and critical success, largely outside of the commercial studio system.

As noted earlier, there is no unified home recording aesthetic, and the diversity even in our limited sample here demonstrates that. But home recording spaces are especially ripe conduits for musical intimacy. Home recordings can convey a greater sense of transparency, simply because they reflect the artist's personal environment. In some cases (as in Daniel Johnston's recordings), the technological limitations of available equipment produce characteristically low-fidelity recordings, but such imperfections can connote a kind of rawness and intimacy that is antithetical to the polished productions of large format, professional recording studios. In other cases (as in the work of Billie Eilish and Finneas O'Connell), the relative freedom of home recording leads to more creative risk taking in ways that challenge accepted conventions in popular music form and production.

The home recordings discussed in this chapter are exemplary of how the home recording environment can yield musically intimate results via making use of a home recording aesthetic. Yet musical intimacy is by no means solely the province of home recordings. Moving beyond this particular recording context, the next two chapters develop and engage a general framework for analyzing intimacy in recorded popular music.

Part II

Text

3

Textual Dimensions of Musical Intimacy

Through ongoing shifts in formats and technological means of both distribution and consumption, recordings continue to be a predominant way that listeners engage with popular music. The preceding chapters discussed the role of the studio space in constructing musical intimacy; while we do not exclude elements of production from this second part of the book, our primary concern here is recordings of popular music as media texts. In this chapter, we identify four primary dimensions of popular music recordings as they relate to musical intimacy: (1) voice, (2) lyrics, (3) song construction and form, and (4) spatiality.

These aesthetic dimensions are affectively charged. Here, we agree with Thompson and Biddle (2013: 16) that music can be understood as a pathway to affective fields. This is underscored by the inherent distributedness of popular music, or in Raymond Williams' (1965) terms, its "structure of feeling." Via broadcast radio, streaming platforms, satellite services, mp3s, and physical formats, recorded popular music remains a wide-reaching component of our culture. And while the expanse of this distributedness can make no claims to a uniform affective experience by its listeners, it underscores the embeddedness of popular music in everyday life. By dissecting the affective and aesthetic dimensions of popular music texts, this chapter works to understand how these texts are constructed to give rise to perceptions of musical intimacy.

Dimension I: Voice

There is a tendency to consider voice and language as inextricably linked. At its most extreme, such a perspective understands the voice as gaining value only inasmuch as it provides a vehicle for linguistic expression. Dolar (2006: 14–15) forcefully argues this position, contending that the voice simply "points toward meaning ... it does not contribute to [meaning] itself." Extending this argument to the musical context, Dolar (2006: 30) understands singing as coming "at the expense of meaning," as "surplus-meaning," and ultimately as turning the voice into a fetish object.

Yet such an extreme view reduces the voice to a mere carrier for language, overlooking its capacity to bear meaning in its own right. The human voice is intricately bound up in matters of identity and expression, and consequently, non-linguistic meaning. To this point, much of the scholarly literature examining the voice centers around questions of humanness and subjectivity. Such philosophical concerns date to at least ancient Greece, as in Aristotle's declaration that "voice is a kind of sound characteristic of what has soul in it; nothing that is without soul utters voice" (420b 5–9).

The notion of voice as a sonic extension of the soul highlights it as a marker of identity, an inherently individualized characteristic. As Frith (1996: 186, 191) observes, "we hear voices as *personally* expressive ... [and] it stands for the person more directly than any other musical device" (emphasis in original). Pursuing this line of argument, Cavarero (2005: 5) outlines what she calls a "vocal ontology of uniqueness," wherein part of what the voice manifests and communicates is "the true, vital, and perceptible uniqueness of the one who emits it." While Barthes (1977: 188) similarly acknowledges the voice's corporeality in his canonic essay, he also argues that not all voices have a grain, as it can be masked or concealed, especially by way of effects processing and the overall mix.[1] By contrast, Cavarero views the voice as always unique precisely because it is bodily. In popular music, the singer's "vocal ontology of uniqueness" serves as an index to their cultivated, public identity—their musical persona (cf. Auslander 2006, 2021). We discuss this notion of musical persona in greater detail in Chapter 6, but it is relevant here in consideration of how the voice alone can suggest that persona, and all of the preexisting associations that a listener may have with it.

Contra Dolar, the voice can carry quite significant meaning beyond linguistic expression. Considerations of volume and tonality, for example, do not simply shape linguistic meaning, but are capable of carrying expressive meaning on their own terms. Moreover, returning to the voice as a marker of identity, consider the connotations that familiar voices can have for the hearer beyond the words that they carry, as in the voices of parents, lovers, or children. It is not the words a mother speaks that provide comfort to her prelinguistic infant child, but the voice itself, wrapped up as it is in her relational identity to the child. In this sense, regardless of what words are spoken, the voice always indicates and reinforces the identity of the speaker, as well as the relationship between speaker and hearer—its history, dynamics, and fundamental nature.

This is not to grant the voice primacy over language. Certainly, we recognize that the voice and language most often work in tandem, the former operating in ways that shape, enhance, or even contradict linguistic meaning. Yet our aim here is simply to acknowledge that voice also has its own unique manner of expressing meaning apart from language. As Peters (2004: 7) puts it, "voices are full of meaning and richness but do not operate according to linguistic codes of signification." Considering these independent values, Paul Zumthor (cited in Cavarero 2005: 5) usefully parses orality from vocality, the former relating to linguistic vocal expressions, while the latter concerns the characteristics, qualities, and functions of voice aside from language. This distinction is useful in analysis of song texts, as it allows us to consider the voice as its own object of analysis, even as it operates alongside linguistic meaning.

The lingering question in this discussion is how precisely the voice can indicate intimacy in popular music. While this will be best illustrated through our analyses in the next chapter, a few key characteristics are worth discussing at the outset. Among these are vocal closeness and tonality. By vocal closeness, we mean simply the sonic proximity of the microphone to the source, allowing for clear vocal articulation of even hushed vocalics. This technique emerged alongside the advent of the electric microphone, aiding the development and popularity of the crooning style in the 1920s, though its application extends well beyond that era and genre. Sonically, vocal closeness contributes to musical intimacy through its subjective effect of placing the listener closer to the singer in relation to the other instruments in the sound-field. In his examination of microphones in film, Rick Altman (1986: 115) refers to this phenomenon as "for-me-ness," a discursivity implied by the fidelity and directionality of the speaker's (or singer's) voice.[2] Of course, these sonic manipulations are to a large extent in the hands of the mixing engineer, but the proximate timbre is generally unmistakable in the final recording. Consider for example the recorded work of Taylor Swift, particularly her pair of 2020 releases, *folklore* and *evermore*. Throughout these albums, Swift's vocal closeness cuts through the standard rock arrangement of bass, drums, guitars, and piano. The recording and mixing of Swift's vocals foreground the breathiness of her delivery and highlight plosive and sibilant vocalizations, as in the songs "'tis the damn season" and "the last great american dynasty"—features of vocal delivery made possible by the microphone, but underscored by production and engineering techniques that allow such soft voices to be placed higher in the mix than other elements.

Volume and timbre are also means by which vocals can cultivate musical intimacy and convey meaning, particularly as it relates to social and cultural norms of emotional expression. A voice that strains to produce a loud, guttural scream may convey anger or urgency, for example, while a soft tone in a lower volume might connote vulnerability, sadness, or seduction. Consider Michael Jackson's characteristic non-linguistic vocalizations ("dah," "hee hee," "hoo," "shamon"), which provide not just rhythmic structure and accent, but also communicate a sense of agency and authority (cf. Johansson 2012). In recorded popular music then, affective meaning can be conveyed autonomously by pure vocality. Most often however, the voice in popular music is also employed to deliver lyrics, and these elements typically work together to convey emotion and intimacy within the song text.

Dimension II: Lyrics

Lyrics provide the most overt layer of meaning in popular music, though as with all media messaging, they are open to multiple, even conflicting readings. Lyrical content can contribute to constructions of musical intimacy in a number of ways. Most explicitly, this comes through emotionally charged lyrics perceived as expressions of the innermost emotions of the singer or songwriter, those that speak to similarly intimate emotions of the listener, or a combination of the two. Song, Dixon, Pearce, and Halpern (2016: 480) suggest that while listeners can perceive emotion through a number of musical qualities and characteristics, lyrics guide listener responses more forcefully than other sonic or structural elements.

Beyond emotion, however, the role of lyrics in constructing musical intimacy is supported and enhanced by other factors embedded in the performer-text-listener triad, including lyrical relationality and sincerity. By lyrical relationality, we refer to how the lyrics position the singer (and/or songwriter) in relation to the listener. Considering the commercial, mass distributed medium of popular music, the sheer scale of an individual singer's expressions directed at a faceless, mass listening audience fundamentally challenges the ability to see this relationality beyond an impersonal supplier-consumer dynamic. In his phenomenology of broadcasting, Scannell (1996: 64) explains that although sound recording and broadcasting address mass audiences, their adoption of interpersonal communication styles allows listeners to experience these transmissions individually, as if they were its sole recipient.

A similar principle operates within popular music, built on the mode of address within the lyrics as being constructed from a first-, second-, or third-person point of view. By design, a third-person perspective (he, she, they) underscores distance, putting listeners into the role of an observing audience. On the other hand, employing first- (I, me, we) and second-person (you, your) points of view can diminish this narrative distance, placing the listener into the subjective position of addressee, directly engaging them with the song's lyrical content. As Glenn Hendler (2020: 12) suggests in such lyrics, "the 'you' being addressed is *explicitly* the (fictional or real) individual loved by the speaker … but in a neat rhetorical trick, the words are *actually* written for the more general 'you' that is their real readership or audience" (emphasis in original). This is not to suggest that in hearing first- and second-person lyrical points of view, listeners fall under the delusion that the singer is speaking to them in a literal sense. Nor do we purport that for listeners to relate to or identify with lyrical content, they must be the subjects of direct address. However, this kind of subjective positioning of the listener can more actively engage them by making lyrical content more relatable, and by drawing them closer to the narrative world of the lyrics.

Regardless of the narrative point of view, lyrics can further cultivate musical intimacy through their perceived sincerity, which is once again tied up with the subjective relationship between singer and listener. Understood as "the hallmark of the personal," sincerity can play a significant role as a conduit for musical intimacy (Scannell 1996: 60). Certainly, sincerity is not performed through lyrics alone, but acts in conjunction with other performative elements including vocal tone and intensity. Moreover, the words that a person sings carry an added weight if listeners perceive them to be coming "from the heart," or true to the performer's self. Here again, a singer's musical persona comes into play. If a singer's musical persona is one that emphasizes authentic and sincere expression (see for example, our discussion of Bruce Springsteen in Chapter 6), lyrical sincerity and musical persona can serve to reinforce one another, especially if the listener has an ongoing, established admiration or fandom of the performer. However, as with musical intimacy, sincerity in popular music trades on perception. In this regard, whether or not Arianna Grande's lyrics are her sincere expressions is far less important than whether audiences *perceive* them as being such; it is of little significance whether she truly believes what she sings, but she can be perceived as sincere if "she *performs as if* she believes what she sings" (cf. Scannell 1996: 67, emphasis added).

We agree with Scannell (1996) that sincerity serves both to authenticate and mediate intimacy in a general sense, and we thus see the performance and perception of sincerity as fundamental to notions of musical intimacy. Yet musical intimacy is not solely the province of lyrics and voice. Formal elements of song construction and form can also play a role, in tandem with or in the absence of vocal and lyrical elements. It is to these compositional elements that we now turn.

Dimension III: Song Construction and Form

As an expressive form, music is often understood as universal, and listeners tend to understand disparate, unfamiliar forms of music through structures of pitch, tone, and emotional expression (Balkwill and Thompson 1999; Castellano, Bharucha and Krumhansl 1984; Kessler, Hansen and Shepard 1984; Oram and Cuddy 1995). At the same time, musical form is culturally specific, even when adopting, borrowing, or outright copying ideas and structures from a different cultural identity or genre. Western European traditions, for example, emphasize harmonic and melodic concepts centered upon structures that often rely on twelve semitones per octave. Within Western traditions, popular song construction and form have been refined, re-worked, and produced with an ever-increasing degree of sophistication for well over a century, coinciding with the technical revolution that gave rise to the modern recording industry.

In music, formal structure is the result of a combination of the interconnectedness of (and interactions between) melody, rhythm, and harmony. In Western European traditions, these musical elements have combined in ways dictated by common practice, genre, geography, technology, and time period. Further, these culturally defined frameworks and conventions aid the construction and implementation of acoustic codes, including those related to structure, affect, and motion (Bharucha, Curtis, and Paroo 2006: 165). These conventions and codes of music form the basic scaffolding from which our discussion of song construction and form originates.

Taken as a whole, the elements of musical form and structure create an inexorable connection with emotive aspects of an engaged listener's potential response to a given piece of music. Although the strength of that connection may be dependent upon the listener's level of musical training, research finds that multiple sonic factors such as "intensity, dynamics, timbre, rhythm and melodic contours are important superficial cues for the iconic representation" of expressiveness, with emotion also playing a role (Tillmann and Bigand 1996; see also Gabrielsson and Lindström 2010; Kawakami, Furukawa, Katahira, Kamiyama, and Okanoya 2012; Laurier, Lartillot, Eerola, and Toiviainen 2009). Yet because such studies typically use classical or uniquely constructed works for their analyses, their implications do not necessarily apply to smaller formal structures mentioned above that are more common to popular music.

As our analytical concern in this book is primarily popular music from the latter half of the twentieth century to present day, our focus is on three types of structural form most commonly found in this music: strophic music (AAA), where the same (or nearly the same) harmonic and melodic structure is repeated; thirty-two-bar song form (AABA), where each section consists of eight-bars, with the B section providing contrast; and verse-chorus form (VC, VCB), where the sections are of roughly equal length, but contrast in harmonic and melodic aspects. These forms have proven to be exceptionally durable, in part due to economic factors. Strophic forms at danceable tempi fit perfectly onto 45 RPM records, for example, which, by the 1950s, had become the preferred format for popular music. If we dig deeper, we find that these forms, while economically viable and efficient, are also incredibly well systematized and cost-effective. For example, the constraints, conventions, and generally accepted forms of popular music structures—including the intentional, calculated repetition of tonal, lyrical, harmonic, melodic, and rhythmic elements—are by their very nature designed to aid in memorization and retention by the listener. This in turn can enhance the impact of popular music's affective qualities, and heighten listener perceptions of musical intimacy through repetitive, sustained engagement with an emotional investment in a piece of music. While musical structure and form provide the construction and progression of a piece of music, the instrumental arrangement and use of musical space are also essential components for helping to establish a particular sonic context.

Dimension IV: Spatiality

As discussed in the previous two chapters, the physical space of musical production contributes directly to its shape and sonic character, be it in a large-format commercial studio or a home recording setup. Treating sound recordings as texts however, two primary levels of spatiality come into play: musical density and phonographic diegesis. Musical density simply refers to the techniques employed by musicians, engineers, and producers to shape and occupy the sonic space within a given recording (e.g., Moore and Martin 2019: 149). A densely mixed pop song, for example, takes full advantage of multitrack recording, layering dozens of individual tracks such that for listeners, mentally parsing out any one of them from the mix may be difficult. "Take My Breath" by The Weeknd (2021) is one example of this production aesthetic. Here, the chorus sections (e.g., 1:19–1:33) exhibit an exceptionally dense mix, featuring multiple vocal layers and harmonies supported by a battery of similarly layered synthesizers. The dense layering of these tracks is such that they become nearly indistinct, blending together to create a dense sonic atmosphere rather than a mix of distinct, identifiably separate tracks.

By contrast, a sparse mix of a solo vocal performance with only acoustic guitar accompaniment foregrounds what little sonic information is present, simultaneously drawing attention to the unfilled sonic space. Such low-density recordings may also increase the likelihood of inadvertent intimacies such as percussive sound of a pick on the guitar strings, the squeal of the player's fingers sliding across the fretboard, or non-vocalic sounds of the singer shaping their lips, mouth, and tongue in order to deliver the desired vocal. To take one example, Logan Farmer's 2020 release *Still No Mother* contains many features that characterize a low-density recording. Utilizing a single microphone and extremely limited production equipment, the album is replete with hushed vocal performances and a faintly fingerpicked acoustic guitar, intimate sonics that are pushed to the foreground by their exposure and lack of instrumental cover.

Spatial considerations in audio recording are further utilized as a means to produce elements of sonic location, distance, and environment for the listener, and also to orient the listener within that environment. For example, the volume and timbre of instruments in a mix, and creative balancing and panning in the sound field all work to present listeners with a particular orientation to those sounds, while inviting them to engage in the sonic interplay between them. Scholars have crafted models for visualizing and analyzing these dynamics of sonic spatiality, variably described as a "sound box" (Dockwray and Moore 2010; Moore and Martin 2001) or "sound stage" (Moylan 2015).

Moore and Martin (2019: 149) concretize these spatial dynamics according to axes of depth (distance), and horizontal (the spectrum of left-center-right provided by stereo sound fields) dimensions. Listeners' perception of these spatial orientations is further enriched by our understanding of real-world sonic environments experienced in everyday life, while those for which we have no such experiential referent "can become utterly surreal" (Brøvig-Hanssen and Danielsen 2013: 71). Peter Gabriel's 2002 album *Up* exemplifies the recording studio's possibilities as an expressive, potentially otherworld-like contributor to expanded sonic spatiality in a musical production. In the opening track "Darkness," Gabriel challenges our perceptions and expectations of how a voice should naturally sound at very close distance, through careful equalization and drastic, even brutal limiting on the vocal to the point of saturation and distortion. This juxtaposition of objective acoustic reality with an alternate sonic space creates a bizarre auditory environment that serves to deepen our connection with the music, the lyrics, and the emotive and intimate impact of the gestalt.

Reverberation, echo, and delay are a few such techniques for sonically representing space. This can simply be the product of the recording space itself, be it accidental or intentional. One notable such example is John Bonham's drum track for Led Zeppelin's "When the Levee Breaks" (1971), which had the drummer playing at the bottom of a stairwell while being miked from the floor above. The result is a booming, reverberant drum track that provides the sonic foundation for the recording and its lyrical sense of foreboding while also giving a clear sense of spatiality.

Importantly, similar effects are often achieved by artificial means, whether as a result of physical acoustics (as with echo chambers common in recording studios since the 1950s), electronic processing (such as the Echoplex tape delay machine, reverb effects pedals, and digital post-production treatments), or strictly acoustic devices. Through the use of spring reverbs, plate reverbs, and actual acoustic chambers or echo chambers, recording engineers and producers sought to enhance, or, in many cases, artificially create a particular sense of space in their work, and such practices became increasingly common by the mid-twentieth century (Doyle 2005: 6). Moylan (2015: 206) notes that through such techniques, constructing a sense of space "may support other elements by delineating musical materials, by adding new dimensions to the unique character of the sound source … and/or by adding to the motion or direction of a musical idea." Specifically, the production element of added reverberation began to take on a more prominent role, becoming considered as important as instrumental and vocal tracks. Producers, musicians, and engineers alike began to understand and implement artificial reverb to enhance sonic spatiality of the song, which can then directly shape the musical intimacy of the recording.

Reverb represents or mimics the interaction of sound waves in their space of production, and can thus be imbued with an array of spatial connotations related to physical spaces (a large gymnasium versus a small, sound-insulated recording booth), distance (more reverb indicating greater distance, less indicating closer proximity), and the relationality between sound's source and its hearer (an authoritative omnipotence, or an ethereal ghostliness) (Sterne 2015: 112). Other technological innovations afforded further means of manipulating sonic space in sound recordings, though at times with an effect of *dis*orienting the sense of sonic space. In recording Miles Davis' *Bitches Brew* (1970) for example, producer Teo Macero and Columbia Records developed a tape machine capable of producing multiple simultaneous delays of varying lengths and times, creating a surreal, disorienting sense of sonic space (Zagorski-Thomas 2018: 863).

Another approach to constructing and manipulating a recording's sonic spatiality involves a variety of techniques that serve to reinforce or disrupt the recording's diegetic space. Drawing from film and literary studies, Walther-Hansen (2015: 37) describes phonographic diegesis as "the perceived temporally connected performance. Sound events in the diegesis simply take place at the same time and the perceived performers can then logically respond to (hear) each other." Walther-Hansen goes on to argue that the diegetic bond is most apparent when it is altered or disrupted. In a particularly illustrative example, Björk's "There's More to Life than This" (1993) places the singer at a party. When the singer retreats to the restroom to lament her boredom (1:36), the sonics of the music shift appropriately—still present, but muffled as if "outside" of the sonic space of the restroom that Björk occupies.[3] The narrative of Biggie Smalls' "Party and Bullshit" (1993) follows the rapper to a party where a fight breaks out in the middle of the third verse. At this point (2:37), an abrupt record scratch stops the music, and is followed by an altercation in the crowd. Above the melee, we hear Biggie's plea to "Chill, yo chill man, chill!" before returning to the narrative and sonics of the verse's conclusion. In a final example, The Ramones' "Do You Remember Rock and Roll Radio" (1980) begins with the static and crosstalk of a scan across the radio dial before settling on the voice of a male disc jockey who introduces the track and returns at its conclusion to back-talk the song. At both ends of the recording, the scanning, speech, and radio sounds are run through high-pass and low-pass filters to mimic the treble-laden sounds of a transistor radio. Examples such as these are clearly the product of deliberate mixing and production techniques. Even so, phonographic diegesis can serve to put listeners into the imagined narrative space of a recording when listeners engage in something akin to suspension of disbelief, or what Brøvig-Hanssen (2013: 17) discusses as "transparent mediation"—a listener's willingness to ignore the mediated, constructed nature of the sonic performance. We return to the concept of transparent mediation in Chapter 5.

Taking musical density and phonographic diegesis into consideration, the construction and use of sonic space in recorded popular music can be closely intertwined with shaping its perceived meaning, and can function in ways that support other dimensions (such as lyrics), or operate independently of them (Kraugerud 2017). The spatial elements inherent in any modern music production can thus be employed as an artistic device, in the service of the interpretive impact of the music, and sonically constructing a sense of musical intimacy.

We make no claims that Voice, Lyrics, Song Construction and Form, and Spatiality are the only possible dimensions through which we might consider intimacy in popular music recordings. However, we do argue that they are the most prominent and thus most productive frameworks for analysis. In elucidating each of the four dimensions above, we provided a series of examples to help illustrate how these dimensions function in recorded music. However, these passing examples are not sufficient to provide depth of analysis or to fully explicate this analytical framework. As such, the following chapter presents analyses of four unique recordings, allowing a more in-depth application of these dimensions of musical intimacy.

4

Analyzing Musical Intimacy

Building on the four dimensions of musical intimacy outlined in Chapter 3, in this chapter we apply the dimensions to four different recordings to actively engage them in analysis. As in the previous chapter, we treat each dimension separately for ease of analysis and comprehension. In practice however, these dimensions are often not discrete, blending and blurring over the course of a given recording. Further, we note at the outset that such analysis is to some degree interpretive. Across a lifetime of consumption, listeners process music through a web of associations that link past listening experience with particular perceptions, understandings, and valuations of music and sound (Dibben 2003). This does not mean that we can or should strive for strict uniformity in how we perceive musical intimacy; the storehouse of personal, associative links that we all maintain ensures some degree of subjectivity in what we perceive as intimate and why. To adopt Gabriel Lubell's (2020: 113) disclaimer in his study of sonic urgency in popular music, we understand that musical intimacy "is not something that can be quantified, and there is no guarantee that two listeners will perceive it at all!" Indeed, another pair of listeners applying our four dimensions to these same recordings could reasonably produce different perceptions of how each recording exhibits musical intimacy (cf. Middleton 1990). Even so, we provide these analyses to demonstrate the four dimensions in action; whether other analysts would produce precisely the same results, the exercise yields specific examples of how composition, performance, engineering, and production can operate in service of constructing musical intimacy in recordings of popular music.

"Blue 7"

Sonny Rollins (1956)[1]

Background

The 12-inch long playing disc became the dominant album format in the 1950s. Compared to the 78 rpm gramophone disc, the LP's larger disc and its slower speed of 33 1/3 rpm resulted in the possibilities of longer (or more) songs per side. Jazz musicians in particular were afforded the opportunity to stretch out in recorded works without feeling the time constraints of prior formats. One such album to take advantage of these looser restrictions was *Saxophone Colossus* (1956), the sixth full-length studio album by saxophonist Sonny Rollins. Notably, the album's eleven-minute closer, "Blue 7," features an extended small group exploration and improvisation made up of eight solo sets, each of which is composed of between one and seven twelve-bar choruses. What we hear throughout this framework in the recording is a full, seemingly live musical performance showcasing solo comments, musical conversations, and thematic developments in their entirety.

In his 1957 review of the album for *Downbeat*, Ralph Gleason (1957) wrote that "Blue 7" was "an especially compelling work ... it is all modern jazz of the first rank." Part of what makes this piece so fascinating are its various constructions of and engagements with musical intimacy, demonstrating that musical intimacy is not solely the domain of recordings that contain vocals and lyrics. On a cursory level, "Blue 7" resembles a fairly typical twelve-bar blues presented within the confines of a jazz quartet. However, focused and active listening reveals the brilliance of the performance and the ensuing production becomes apparent, bringing to light this piece's effective and illustrative depiction of all four of the dimensions of musical intimacy.

Dimension I: Voice

Although there is no vocalist on "Blue 7," there are multiple instrumental voices that contribute to the overall aesthetic impact of the piece. In any musical ensemble, be it a rock group or a symphony orchestra, the various musical instruments can be said to be in conversation, building toward the whole of the piece. A small jazz combo arguably affords a uniquely intimate musical dialogue; as in interpersonal conversations, fewer participants allow for increased engagement from each individual, and a more intimate exchange. This is the nature of the dialogue showcased throughout "Blue 7."

In addition to Rollins on tenor saxophone, the recording includes Tommy Flanagan on piano, Doug Watkins on bass, and Max Roach on drums. Together, the players create a texture that heightens the impact of the instrumental voices in the construction of musical intimacy. One of the most pronounced aspects of these instrumental voices, particularly as the song progresses through the solos, is the thread of continuity and conversation between the soloists. This aesthetic of continuity is common among jazz musicians who are adept at the art of improvisation, and the resultant music often carries melodic, rhythmic, and harmonic fragments or ideas from a previous solo, as a form of musical expression and conversation. The five chorus sections of Solo Set 1 demonstrate this idea of instrumental conversation well.

The first chorus of Solo Set 1 (1:07–1:27) includes a musical conversation that is primarily between tenor sax and piano. In a sense, what we hear is a question-answer musical construction. Rollins plays a solo idea—a melodic motif, or a fragment from the head—and Flanagan answers it with a harmonic, chordal flourish that enhances the musical fabric and solidifies the harmonic direction of the song. The two musicians rarely overlap each other's playing. The second chorus of Solo Set 1 (1:28–1:49) is slightly more energetic. Flanagan's piano commentary is more active, which mirrors Rollins' increasingly busy solo. Concerning another player on "Blue 7," it is worth pointing out that drummer Max Roach's toms are tuned roughly to Db, Gb, and A (Kenfield 1995: 166). While not necessarily a chord, this tuning allows the toms to blend well with the other tonal instruments, emphasized by Roach's melodic approach to fill on the recording. An illustration of the effectiveness of this approach occurs when Roach inserts himself into the musical dialogue with a well-placed tom-tom fill near the end of the chorus (1:36).[2]

Representing essentially the midpoint of Solo Set 1, Chorus 3 (1:50–2:10) recalls the musical texture of Chorus 1. Flanagan's angular harmonic comments, in response to Rollins' tenor sax, are more subdued, and that mirrors Rollins' solo in these twelve bars. Rollins' tenor solo begins to become somewhat more agitated in Chorus 4 of Solo Set 1 (2:11–2:32). Here, he plays in a higher register than in previous choruses with an accompanying increased note density, contributing to a palpable increase in energy. Flanagan's piano part follows suit, playing a bit louder while incorporating a higher register. Finally, Chorus 5 in Solo Set 1 (2:33–2:53) serves a dual purpose in "Blue 7."

It is the culminating chorus in Rollins' first set of five choruses, and it also becomes a transition to Solo Set 2, which features Tommy Flanagan soloing for three twelve-bar choruses. Throughout the twelve bars of Chorus 5 in Solo Set 1, we hear the continued musical conversation between Rollins and Flanagan; Flanagan's dynamic level increases noticeably in this section, which provides a smooth transition into his upcoming solo while subtly drawing our focus from the tenor sax solo to the upcoming three-chorus piano solo in Solo Set 2.

Throughout "Blue 7" and specifically in the instrumental solos, it is clear that the musicians are listening to each other and adding comments and elaborations to melodic or rhythmic fragments of earlier solos. In particular, Rollins' tenor saxophone solos throughout the piece have inspired spirited debate among musicologists and jazz historians as to whether the thematic content of the solos is connected throughout, is a product of Rollins' musical language at the time, or both. Givan (2014: 168) attempts to reconcile these perspectives, arguing that "from a purely listener-oriented standpoint, we can generally gain richer insights by interpreting them as spontaneous hypostatizations of their creators' stylistic idioms rather than as discrete onetime events." Furthermore, timbral, textural, and various distance cues in the actual recording contribute a sense of sonic realism to the piece and serve to underscore and support the audible nature of the dialogic bonds between the musicians, as we discuss below.

Improvisation in jazz music is an unquestionably a defining characteristic of the genre, and it is this aspect which informs and supports the discussion of the voice dimension in "Blue 7." From a performer's perspective, improvisation sets the boundaries for what is and what is not musically possible; these boundaries are fluid, oftentimes depending on the song, the style, and the fellow musicians. Importantly, effective improvisation relies not only on musical knowledge, but also on dynamics between players. Such a collective activity of spontaneous musical exchange requires a certain consciousness of making musical statements and responding to those of other players. These interpersonal dynamics have led to conceptualizing improvisation as a conversation or dialogue between players and such an understanding emphasizes the perceptive and intimate relational dynamics between players (Berliner 1994; McAuliffe 2021; Monson 1996; Sawyer 2005). This kind of intimate conversation is on full display in the improvised sections of "Blue 7." An intriguing aspect of the solo choruses in the recording lies in the connection and communication between the musicians through their solos as the piece progresses, at once synthesizing real-time influences as a result of the preceding solo(s) with the individual histories brought to bear as a jazz musician in the 1950s. That is, the intricate conversation evident between the playing of Rollins, Flanagan, Watkins, and Roach sets up an intimate dynamic between each instrument, but also between the players themselves, as they collectively intuit and carry on the largely improvised conversation with one another.

Dimension II: Lyrics

"Blue 7" is an instrumental piece, so there is no direct discussion of Dimension II in this analysis. However, in relation to the above discussion of voice and instrumental dialogue, *lyrics* should not be conflated with *lyricism*. Lyricism is a term often used by jazz critics and musicologists to denote a fluidity of melodic ideas in a particular performance or solo. The term may be applied on a number of levels, including the perspective of an overall piece, an analysis of some inner working of the ensemble, or to a specific solo or set of solos.

Fluidity itself often describes a particular performance or solo, and revolves around the similarity between the performance in question and a comparable vocal performance. Fluidity in soloing begets musical dialogue, as witnessed by the apparent ease with which a virtuoso musician like Sonny Rollins can non-verbally communicate his message to the other musicians in the group and to the listener. Furthermore, Lowney (2015: 100) notes that "improvisation is frequently associated with freedom and spontaneity, but the process of improvising also involves an active engagement with traditional musical and cultural practices."

It is this integration of the musicians' life experiences, musical training, and the need to communicate their message that brings the dual concepts of lyricism and dialogue back to the concept of musical intimacy within an instrumental piece. Especially in the context of a jazz solo, heightened musical dialog and lyricism strengthen the impact of the piece, the solo, and its message, all working together to enhance the emotional and aesthetic qualities of the music. In the context of this analysis, the lyrical aspects of the piece are intertwined with aspects of its structure and sonic spatiality, explored in greater depth and detail under Dimensions III and IV below.

Dimension III: Song Construction and Form

"Blue 7" is a relatively standard twelve-bar blues, albeit with several modifications to the expected, standard form. Structurally, the primary feature of the recording is its eight sets of individual solos, each of which is composed of between one and seven twelve-bar sections, known in jazz parlance as choruses. This recording's complex structure does not itself connote musical intimacy, although structural elements throughout the song do enhance or give rise to instances of musical intimacy in the other three dimensions. One such example are the inadvertent intimacies in Solo Set 3 (3:59–6:21), which covers seven twelve-bar choruses featuring Max Roach on drums. Here, there are audible squeaks and rattles coming from Max Roach's solo drum kit, most evident in Chorus 5 (5:23–5:42).

Table 1 The Structure of "Blue 7".

Doug Watkins, bass	Chorus 1 0:02	Chorus 2 0:24					
Head	0:45						
SOLO SET 1 Sonny Rollins, tenor sax	Chorus 1 1:07	Chorus 2 1:28	Chorus 3 1:50	Chorus 4 2:11	Chorus 5 2:33		
SOLO SET 2 Tommy Flanagan, piano	Chorus 1 2:54	Chorus 2 3:16	Chorus 3 3:37				
SOLO SET 3 Max Roach, drums	Chorus 1 3:59	Chorus 2 4:20	Chorus 3 4:41	Chorus 4 5:02	Chorus 5 5:23 (audible squeaks)	Chorus 6 5:43	Chorus 7 6:03
SOLO SET 4 Sonny Rollins, tenor sax	Chorus 1 6:22	Chorus 2 6:43	Chorus 3 7:04	Chorus 4 7:25	Chorus 5 7:46		
SOLO SET 5 Tommy Flanagan, piano	Chorus 1 8:08						
4-bar extension (bass)	8:29						
SOLO SET 6 Doug Watkins, bass	Chorus 1 8:38	Chorus 2 8:59					
SOLO SET 7 Trading 4s (Rollins, Roach)	Chorus 1 9:21	Chorus 2 9:41					
SOLO SET 8 Sonny Rollins, tenor sax	Chorus 1 10:02	Chorus 2 10:23	Chorus 3 10:45				

Note: A chorus equals twelve measures.

As discussed in Chapter 1, mid-century drum hardware was especially prone to producing such inadvertent intimacies. Yet in addition to Van Gelder's close microphone placement, it is the intense rhythmic structure of Roach's playing in these choruses that produces the squeaks and rattles emanating from his drumkit.

Throughout the song, but particularly in his solo choruses, Roach's playing is at once keenly sensitive to the other musicians and intimately expressive on his own instrument. In Chorus 2 of Solo Set 3 (4:20–4:40), Roach makes extensive use of the two-over-three polyrhythm (see Figure 1) to further outline and enhance not only the formal structure, but rhythmic ideas taken from Rollins' first and second choruses in Solo Set 1. Throughout Roach's choruses, we hear bits and pieces of both Rollins' and Flanagan's previous solos, evincing the ongoing, intimate conversation between musical voices described above.

The structure and form of Solo Set 7 (9:21–10:01) similarly facilitate the intimate instrumental dialogue between players. Specifically, Solo Set 7 consists of two twelve-bar choruses wherein Rollins and Roach "trade fours," or alternate four measure sections. Trading fours is a highly interactive form of conversation between players, with each directly responding to the other. The exercise is especially interesting when played over a twelve-bar blues form due to its asymmetry; in one chorus, you will hear one of the two soloists twice; the first soloist takes bars 1–4, the second soloist takes bars 5–8, and the first soloist returns for bars 9–12. In the case of "Blue 7," Rollins and Roach ultimately play an equal amount of "fours" throughout the twenty-four bars of both Chorus 1 and 2. In other words, through the lens of trading fours, Solo Set 7 is composed of six four-bar chunks, divided into two twelve-bar choruses; Rollins and Roach alternate their solos, giving them both three four-bar solos. In essence then, the order of solos is: Rollins-Roach-Rollins-Roach-Rollins-Roach. As a result, this set of trading fours is one of the more explicit instances of the musicians in "Blue 7" directly engaging in musical dialogue, an intimate exchange afforded by the intimacy of the quartet, and the very structure of the composition.

Figure 1 2 Over 3 Rhythm.

Critic Gunther Schuller (1958) provides a comprehensive examination of the structural and tonal form of "Blue 7," and specifically, how the solo sections are examples not just of improvisation, but of thematic development that in some details borrow, refine, and extend classical techniques used in formal structures like theme and variations. Schuller's term for this compositional technique was extemporization: a real-time combination of improvisation and composition. Schuller has been roundly criticized for not considering Rollins' environment or training in his analysis. However, his examination, observation, and insights into how the thematic development in Rollins' solos can be seen to be (at least partially) rooted in Western European Art Music form a basis from which we can extrapolate the further melodic, harmonic, and rhythmic connections across these solos—connections that unify the musical message and amplify the aspects of musical intimacy that are contained within.

Dimension IV: Spatiality

The aural impression of space in "Blue 7" occurs on multiple sonic, aesthetic, and perceptual levels. Of note here is the physically intimate space where "Blue 7" (and all of *Saxophone Colossus*) was recorded: Rudy Van Gelder's relatively small, residential studio in Hackensack, New Jersey. Noting their son's interest in audio recording, Van Gelder's parents designed their Hackensack home with such activity in mind. In essence, a spare bedroom was architecturally fitted to serve as a control room, while the living room functioned as the recording space. With its ten-foot-high ceiling and adjoining hallways and archways, the latter facilitated sonic representations of spatiality and room reverberation in Van Gelder's early recordings (Skea 2001: 57). In addition to its small size and domestic character, the design features of Van Gelder's Hackensack studio provided a sonic canvas for the intimate musical conversation described above.

In addition to the studio itself, the perception of space in "Blue 7" is to a large degree a result of Van Gelder's recording techniques, including microphone choice, placement, and the application of artificial reverb. Throughout, we hear artificial reverberation applied to primarily one instrument at a time. Rather than disorienting the listener's sense of sonic space, this addition of reverb fuses elements of the recording environment with instruments "to create an overall timbre to the sound, and also to provide the illusion of its placement in a unique physical space" (Moylan 2009: 2). Importantly, in recording "Blue 7," Van Gelder manipulated reverb's sonic characteristics to complement, support, and enhance the musical ideas of each soloist. Van Gelder also adapted and modified his microphones so that he could place them much closer to each instrument, producing what Crooks (2012: 4) describes as a "sonic palette that is engaged with as real, but is in fact unreal or hyperreal."

This recording features only the individual instruments of the quartet: tenor saxophone, piano, bass, and drums. It is thus not an especially dense recording, nor is it sparse. Throughout, the limitation of four instruments lends a fair amount of openness to the recording, and matters of musical density are primarily engaged through the instruments' notational and rhythmic activity. Chorus 3 of Solo Set 4 (7:04–7:25), for example, begins with a noticeable abundance of sonic space on account of less intense rhythmic activity overall. In contrast, the concluding three twelve-bar choruses in Solo Set 1 (1:50–2:53) feature a rising ensemble intensity especially in Choruses 3 and 4. As the dynamics and intensity increase (such as Rollins' increased note density in Chorus 4 (2:11–2:31)), the decay time of the reverb is audibly shorter. This shortened reverb tail is necessary in part because Rollins' playing is more rapid, and in Chorus 4, the ensemble's overall dynamic level is noticeably louder. That is, whereas Van Gelder uses reverb to both connote and fill space, the increased density of the playing in this section requires a reduction in reverb to open up more sonic space for the instruments. Chorus 5 in Solo Set 4 (7:46–8:07) features a similar occurrence. This solo begins with an energy that is slightly more frenetic than sections that immediately precede it, along with a quicker tempo building to an eventual climax. As in Chorus 4 in Solo Set 1, the artificial reverb decreases inversely with the density and intensity of the ensemble.

In addition, the drier, more upfront sound produced by reverb reduction tends to put the soloist in closer sonic proximity to the listener as in Rollins' saxophone at Solo Set 4 Chorus 1 (6:22–6:43); a similar effect occurs in Solo Set 4 Chorus 3 (7:04–7:21). For nearly the first two measures of this chorus, Flanagan's piano is silent, leaving only drums, bass, and tenor sax. The reduced instrumentation and resulting quieter dynamic level, coupled with the increased presence of Rollins' reed sound, pushes the tenor saxophone to the forefront of the mix. Due to this, Rollins seems sonically much closer to the listener, which in turn contributes to a heightened sense of musical intimacy.

From a spatial perspective, "Blue 7" includes a number of inadvertent intimacies as well. In addition to the squeaks and rattles from Roach's drum kit mentioned earlier, a great deal of reed sound from Rollins' saxophone is also evident throughout, likely facilitated by recording at high levels through close microphone placement. This is audible in Solo Sets 1 (1:07–2:53), 4 (6:22–8:07), and 8 (10:02–end) for example. This "breathiness" of Rollins' playing suggests a close proximity between his horn and the listener. The reed sound's presence is not constant, however. As Solo Set 4 proceeds for example (6:22–8:07), we hear Rollins gradually settle back into the mix as the prominence of reed sound diminishes in favor of a more overall body, or developed, sound from his saxophone. While the presence of reed sound may connote physical proximity and the intimate studio space, its shifting presence also evokes movement, engaging listener perceptions of a dynamic spatial relation to Rollins' horn on the sound stage.

Van Gelder's selective application of reverb also facilitates this sense of movement within the sonic field. In Solo Set 1, for example, the first two notes of the solo (1:07–1:11) have more reverb, which then audibly recedes, becoming drier in texture. This has the sonic effect of bringing the saxophone from the background or distance to the fore. Van Gelder plays with this sonic shifting throughout to highlight certain instruments at certain times in the recording, while also enabling movement and proximity to promote spatial intimacy as well as musical dialogue. The sonic shifting between instruments moving between the background and foreground in this sense recalls a tradition of live jazz performances, where individual musicians might step out in front of the combo during their solo passages. This tactic supports Van Gelder's attention to detail regarding sonic space, which he often conceptualized as "a soundstage in which listeners could visualize the musicians" (RVG Legacy 2021). Van Gelder's inclusion and use of artificial reverb in this way can be understood to be as much of an instrument as Flanagan's piano accompaniment, as both are commenting on and reacting to the phrasing and content of the individual players' solos. Overall, these non-static mix elements of movement, sonic proximity, and fluctuations in density can serve to heighten listener engagement and interest. When we hear mix elements moving in the sound-field, either laterally (if stereo) or front to back through mid- to high-frequency addition or removal, these constant shifts in dynamics are demanding of our attention, and thus can then keep listeners interested and engaged in the material.

"Blue 7" is a complex piece, and in many respects unique among the other recordings analyzed in this chapter in that it is the only instrumental selection that we have included. Particularly when discussions of musical intimacy emphasize affective and emotional elements, lyrical expression serves as a rich source of such material. But as our analysis of "Blue 7" demonstrates, instrumental works can certainly exhibit musical intimacy, and do so in ways that are fundamentally different from vocal recordings. "Blue 7" is also unique among our sample in that the four dimensions of musical intimacy are much more intricately intertwined, and difficult to parse out as distinct elements. Perhaps more than any other recording in our sample then, "Blue 7" demonstrates the ways that these four dimensions interact and shape each other to develop a cumulatively intimate, affective listening experience.

"How Come U Don't Call Me Anymore"

Prince (1982)

Background

Recorded at Hollywood's Sunset Sound studios during the sessions for his *1999* album (1982), Prince initially issued "How Come U Don't Call Me Anymore" as the non-album B-side to the "1999" single in September 1983 (Nilsen et al. 2004: 36, 428). Of his catalog, the *1999* album is perhaps most emblematic of the "Minneapolis Sound" that became associated with Prince and his contemporaries, driven by layers of synthesizers and the Linn LM-1 drum machine. "How Come U Don't Call Me Anymore," on the other hand, is a solo piano and vocal performance with minimal overdubs. The stark contrast between these sonic palates was perhaps the justification for relegating "How Come U Don't Call Me Anymore" to a B-side. Although Prince's original recording received scant commercial attention at the time of its release, "How Come U Don't Call Me Anymore" subsequently became a staple of his live shows, and found success via cover versions recorded by Stephanie Mills (1983), Joshua Redman (1998), David McMurray (1999), and Alicia Keys (2001).

Dimension I: Voice

Prince's vocal performance is arguably the dominant feature of "How Come U Don't Call Me Anymore." Mixed to the center, Prince's lead vocal becomes a focal point of attention, reinforced by the quality of the vocal performance itself. Prince utilizes his falsetto register throughout the track, generally coming across as soft and non-abrasive in tone, allowing for smooth *glissandi* between notes.[3] Particularly coming through a male voice, the falsetto here can connote tenderness and sensitivity, challenging as it does stereotypical notions of masculinity as simultaneously exhibiting strength while shielding vulnerability.

There are moments of contrast however, where Prince more forcefully projects his falsetto into a strained, abrasive scream as he sings (as at 1:45, 2:07, and 2:52). A hallmark of Prince's vocal style throughout his career, the screaming falsetto in "How Come U Don't Call Me Anymore" is deployed to deliver lyrics that find the protagonist especially pleading, an emphasis on the urgency and frustration of his loneliness (as at 1:44–1:50, 2:07–2:14, and 2:51–2:54). While these passages may not reflect the proximal intimacy of the softer vocal runs, they do underscore the intensity of yearning to reclaim romantic intimacy with the addressee; they may also be read as an urgency born out of the *lack* of intimacy.

Equally as important as the range of Prince's vocal delivery in the song are the dynamics facilitated by his use of the microphone. While little information is available about the session itself, the finished recording suggests close miking of Prince's vocals, capturing a number of utterances that would otherwise be barely audible, from vocable accents to spoken lines and phrases that Prince seemingly utters under his breath (as at 1:31, 1:54–1:55, and 2:04–2:06). Prince's vocal closeness here recalls Altman's (1992: 61–2, 250; see also Altman 1985 and 1986) notion of "for-me-ness," where recorded sound is seemingly "directed straight toward me from relatively close up." Despite the dynamic shifts between these more hushed utterances and the screams mentioned above, there is a consistency in how Prince's voice is situated within the song's final mix; we hear the subtleties of the quieter passages clearly; yet, the louder runs are not at all distorted or "in the red." Such consistency suggests attention to these vocal dynamics in the recording process, both in terms of Prince's consideration of his physical positioning to the microphone while singing (moving in for the softer pieces, leaning back or away for the louder runs) and in a similar attention to achieving this consistency through attentive mixing (mixing the softer runs at a slightly higher level, and similarly pulling back on the louder segments). As with much popular music, Prince's vocal performance in "How Come U Don't Call Me Anymore" is a vehicle for linguistic expression via lyrics, with each of these codependent elements serving to reinforce the other and the broader construction of intimacy within the recording.

Dimension II: Lyrics

Throughout Prince's oeuvre, communication technology serves as a recurrent narrative device to convey a sense of romantic intimacy. While later work made narrative use of digital and virtual communication technologies, his 1980s material includes a number of pieces that fit into a long history of "phone songs" in popular music. In these songs, the telephone serves as a somatic marker—a sensory image to which we attach (or "mark") affective associations; in other words, somatic markers are adaptive mental shortcuts that we develop to process the sensory world (Damasio 1994: 174). Although somatic markers are driven by personal experience, certain associations may be common enough to operate as cultural codes, as is the case of the telephone as a platform for intimate encounters. To that point, Glenna Matthews (1993: 756) argues that in the twentieth century, the telephone was second only to face-to-face communication as a means of communicating emotional intimacy.

On its face, the telephone would seem to be the antithesis of intimacy. By design, users are geographically distant, and interaction is mediated by an impersonal technological interface. Yet in collapsing distance, the phone affords intimacy despite physical separation. The interface in fact provides a sensory proximity: we hold one end close to our mouth, the other nestled against our ear as if we were "speaking directly and immediately into each others' ears" (Thompson 2004: 235). While Chion (1999: 63) notes that such "a vocal intimacy ... is rarely encountered in social life," Colton (2014) argues for a symbolic parity between the telephone and the microphone as receptors and transmitters of intimate communication. She goes on to argue that in phone songs such as "How Come U Don't Call Me Anymore," "the microphone represents the communication technology of the telephone, while also acting to transmit the sound of that conversation to the audience. The intimacy of a telephone conversation can therefore be read from the intimacy of the recorded mix" (Colton 2014: 74–5).

In "How Come U Don't Call Me Anymore," Prince's lyrics integrate mediated communication to evoke intimacy and desire, eros and failed connection. The lyrics directly address a former lover. As he reminisces about their emotionally and physically intimate relationship, Prince questions, "If what we had was good, How come you don't call me anymore?" As the song progresses, Prince's pleas for his lover become more impassioned (enhanced by an increasingly intense vocal strain, as noted above). These pleas continue through the song's fadeout (3:25–3:54), though the vocal intensity here diminishes somewhat, as if the singer is resigning himself to not reconnecting with his former lover.

Surveying the history of "phone songs" in popular music, Colton (2014: 69) outlines the typical gender dynamics represented in the lyrics of this body of work. Most often, such songs depict a male caller pursuing a female recipient, showcasing "the notion of the girl answering the telephone as a signal to her suitor of his likely sexual conquest, and her ignoring of the call as sexually frustrating." "How Come U Don't Call Me Anymore" reverses this script, with the forlorn male protagonist anxiously waiting upon his female ex-lover.[4] As with many of Prince's most phone-centric songs, "How Come U Don't Call Me Anymore" presents a narrative of failed connection, depicting precisely the emotional and sexual frustration that Colton outlines. As Peters (1999: 200) puts it in his discussion of telephony, "Waiting for a call that never comes exemplifies not only the loneliness of the neglected lover, but the whole problem of how to know that one has made contact at all." In other words, unanswered calls yield unrequited love—an erotic failure. As a somatic marker, the telephone here serves as the potential remedy for Prince's tortured yearning and loneliness. He pleads not for sexual contact, embrace, or even physical presence, but simply for his estranged lover to "just pick up the phone." Unable to complete the telephonic circuit, he is left alone with only a picture beside his bed—itself an intimate space.

Cummings (2020: 167) notes that throughout his vast catalog, many of Prince's lyrics "are written as conversations with the listener." "How Come U Don't Call Me Anymore" provides an example, delivering its lyrical narrative via combined first- (I, we, our) and second-person (you) points of view. Both perspectives facilitate the construction of intimacy, albeit through different means. The first-person perspective here gives listeners access to the intimate, emotional expressions of the singer, while the second-person perspective places the listener in the subject position of the addressee. While few would believe Prince is singing to them personally, this mode of address invites us into an emotional space that arguably strengthens the song's overall emotional resonance, calling on the listener to empathize with Prince's impassioned pleas for telephonic contact. Taken together, the confessional first-person perspective and the address of the second-person perspective combine to underscore overtures to sincerity in the lyrics, which can further strengthen musical intimacy as discussed in Chapter 3.

Dimension III: Song Construction and Form

With a runtime of approximately three minutes and fifty-five seconds, "How Come U Don't Call Me Anymore" begins with an eight-bar introduction into a sixteen-bar verse, followed by an eight-bar chorus. This repeats through a second verse and chorus before contrasting with an abbreviated six-bar bridge, concluding with an eight-bar outro that completes a fade-out on the first beat of the ninth bar.

The melodic structure of the piece emphasizes a cyclical progression. The main riff is a repeating, two-bar motif that breaks to descend into the chorus structure after the verses, briefly returns to connect the second chorus and the bridge, and finally reemerges for the duration of the outro. The heavy repetition of this two-bar sequence and its relative simplicity facilitates the listener's memorization or ease of familiarity with the song's basic melodic contour, emphasizing groove and feel as opposed to complicated technical intricacies of composition.

Even as this two-bar phrase cycles through repetition, Prince slightly alters the rhythm and dynamics of his piano playing throughout, particularly as to which beats he chooses to accent, and through the use of syncopation. For example, in some cases he stresses the first down beat (as at 0:00), at others the "and" of the fourth beat (as at 0:05 and 0:17), or the "and" of the second beat (as at 0:12). These and other dynamic alterations introduce slight variations within the otherwise repetitive melodic structure, which can help to maintain listener interest.

In the broader structure of the song, there are clear dynamic shifts between the verse and chorus sections. While the piano dynamics are relatively soft in the verse, they are noticeably louder in the chorus (1:08–1:32; 2:19–2:43), and even more so in the bridge section (2:42–2:58). These passages of louder dynamic piano playing in the bridge reflect the heightened fervency, and more forceful dynamics evidenced by the increased vocal and lyrical intensity of these sections. In the chorus for example, Prince sings a contrasting melody from the verse, and with a bit more projection than in the verses. The bridge section features Prince's most intense vocal delivery in terms of dynamics, timbre, and grain; this section finds his voice strained and roughly textured as he screams while still in his falsetto range. Notably, these are also the more emotionally expressive lyrical sections in "How Come U Don't Call Me Anymore." The song's dynamics are at their loudest just as the vocals are also at their most urgent, all while the lyrics reach their emotional peak. In short, the most emotionally potent portions of these three dimensions converge in the chorus and bridge of the song, amplifying the overall affective qualities of the recording. The song's formal structure and seemingly improvisatory yet meticulously structured dynamics also contribute to how the fourth dimension of spatiality is represented in the recording.

Dimension IV: Spatiality

Two factors are especially relevant regarding the spatiality of "How Come U Don't Call Me Anymore." The first of these is musical density. The recording is sparse, featuring only Prince's vocal, piano, overdubbed background vocals (also by Prince), and the sound of his foot keeping time, likely on one of the piano's foot pedals. Save for the isolated finger snap accenting the transition into the first chorus, these four elements comprise the entirety of the recording's distinct aural components. This minimalism allows for a great deal of sonic space, particularly within the verses. Here, each sonic element—voice, piano, foot—has room to breathe, with neither drowning out the other. Arguably, Prince is also leveraging this sonic space by stretching the tempo (almost *rubato* in pace) and using "the space between the notes" as an emotive element as well. In short, this sense of sonic space spotlights even minor elements of the recording (the accented dynamics of the piano playing, the foot, the close miked vocals), granting each a sense of importance that would otherwise be lost in a more dense, active arrangement. Consider for example cover versions of the song such as those by Stephanie Mills (1983) and Alicia Keys (2002). Both feature a greater level of musical density than Prince's original, along with a more polished production aesthetic. These characteristics make for a successful commercial recording, but significantly diminish the sense of intimacy constructed by the track's sonic spatiality.

The second noteworthy element as regards spatiality in "How Come U Don't Call Me Anymore" is the apparently artificial reverb on Prince's vocal track.[5] This vocal reverb not only creates a sense of a physical space where such acoustics would naturally occur (a large, empty room), but also underscores the emotional isolation of the narrative. That is, the excessive vocal reverb emphasizes that Prince's pleas fail to connect with the lover he desires; the only voice he is able to hear in response are the reverberations of his own. Within the recording, the moments where vocal reverb is most noticeable are also those where lyrics and vocal increase in their intensity, creating a synergy of these three components in their sonic emphasis (e.g., 1:44–1:50, 2:07–2:13, 2:43–3:02). These two elements of sonic spatiality—the song's low musical density and its heavy vocal reverb—reinforce each other. The vocal reverb is especially notable because the mix is so sparse; this vocal effect that connotes an open, reverberant space is prominent because there are simply not many elements competing for sonic space within the mix.

In "How Come U Don't Call Me Anymore," Prince and engineer Peggy McCreary crafted a recording whose lyrical, compositional, and performative components all work to construct a sonic proximity to Prince as he spins his desperate plea for a lost lover's telephone call. Through its use of first- and second-person address, the lyrics of "How Come U Don't Call Me Anymore" speak directly to the listener. As Colton (2014: 75) argues of "phone songs," "the listener occupies a double subjectivity: both an observer of a song 'about' a relationship, and as the individual receiver of the call, a direct line from the singer." "How Come U Don't Call Me Anymore" operates in precisely this fashion, presenting a dually constructed sense of musical intimacy that is at once diegetic (relayed through lyrical narrative) and non-diegetic (the intimacy constructed between Prince and his listening audience). For all of these reasons, Prince's "How Come U Don't Call Me Anymore" is a particularly vibrant example of musical intimacy in recorded popular music.

"Ain't No Grave"

Johnny Cash (2010)

Background

Although it is possible that some version of "Ain't No Grave" was in circulation among folk and gospel musicians much earlier, the apocryphal story has it that Brother Claude Ely wrote the song in 1934 when, at the age of twelve, he was diagnosed with tuberculosis, and expected not to survive. While bedridden, an uncle lent Ely a guitar as a means to pass the time. As the story goes, his family gathered around the bed to pray for his recovery, at which Ely sprang from bed to declare, "I'm not going to die!" and began to sing what would become "Ain't No Grave." Ely survived the disease, which along with the song, he and his family attributed to God answering their prayers (Ely 2010: xx–xxi; Richman and Freemark 2011).[6]

Ely was not the first to record the song, however. That distinction goes to Bozie Sturdivant and the Silent Grove Baptist Church Choir, as recorded by Alan Lomax and Lewis Jones for the Library of Congress in 1942 (Library of Congress, National Recording Preservation Board). Although Sturdivant's recording suffers fidelity issues given its age, it is a solo acapella rendition with minimal accompaniment from others in the choir, moderate in tempo, and mournful in tone. A 1947 recording by Sister Rosetta Tharpe brings the song into a major key with a more up-tempo gospel/r&b arrangement. Ely did not commit his own rendition to tape until 1953. Recorded live during a Pentecostal revival service, the entire musical aesthetic of Ely's recording could not be more different from Cash's later interpretation. Set in G Major, with a moderately quick tempo, Ely's version exudes an enthusiastic energy, due primarily to the full ensemble, the *forte* dynamic level, and the exuberance typically found in a live church performance. Subsequent recordings tended to replicate these characteristics of Ely's version, as in those by The Singing Cookes (1980) and Russ Taff (1989), among others.

By contrast, Cash's recording transposes the song into the key of A minor, reframing the song in a somber, meditative musical aesthetic. Likely due to Cash's popularity, as well as his version's use in a number of film and television productions,[7] further renditions of "Ain't No Grave" tend to use his recording as the template, following the generally darker tone and more moderate tempo, as in recordings by Scott Lucas and the Married Men (2012), Tom Jones (2015), Wilson Banjo Company (2017), and Renee Elise Goldbury (2018).

Cash's version of the song is the opening track on *American VI: Ain't No Grave*, recorded shortly before his death in 2003, and posthumously released in 2010. The album was the culmination of a decade's worth of sessions with producer Rick Rubin, dating back to 1994's *American Recordings*. *American VI*, and in particular the title track, showcase Cash's voice at the time where he was in the shadow of what he knew was his impending death. In 1997, Cash was diagnosed with Shy-Drager syndrome, a misdiagnosis that in 2001 was changed to autonomic neuropathy, an affliction that affects the nervous system (Dansby 2001). As an elderly, ailing widower, the context of Cash's personal life at this time colors his rendition of "Ain't No Grave," making it tempting to read the piece as a swan song.

In addition to this performance finding Cash very near the end of his life, the music on *American VI* was recorded as often as possible in non-traditional spaces, including Cash's cabin and Rick Rubin's living room. Certainly, the small, idiosyncratic, and personal spaces used in these sessions lend a sonic intimacy to the resultant tracks that is supported and enhanced by the genuine, raw performances and sparse, spacious production aesthetic. These and other factors contribute to a particular presentation of musical intimacy at the hands of Cash and Rubin, as analysis through our four dimensions demonstrates.

Dimension I: Voice

In "Ain't No Grave," Cash's voice is the most prominent instrument in the mix. There are no vocal layers, harmonies, or other production elements, save for moderate compression and equalization. This is in line with the vocal production and overall aesthetic of the *American Recordings* series, and a particular point of focus in Rubin's production, which emphasized "being able to really hear the singer in a personal way, almost to feel like they're in the room with you. Historically the way vocals have been treated is with a reverberant effect that kind of makes them larger than life. I prefer more of a documentary approach where it's more intimate" ("Rick Rubin" 2021). To achieve this in "Ain't No Grave," Cash's vocal track is placed upfront in the mix, clearly higher in level than the other tracks occupying the same central sonic space: primarily, the percussive foot stomps and chain rattles. There is also a vocal closeness throughout the recording, on account of the voice's placement and its wider frequency content, particularly in the higher frequencies. High-frequency content contributes directly to our perception of proximity to a source; as when we are physically close to a sound source, the high frequency content will be more abundant. As the source moves away, the higher frequencies of the source will attenuate approximately four times faster than lower frequencies. Recording engineers use this acoustic phenomenon to simulate depth in stereo recordings, and this is exactly what we hear in the beginning of "Ain't No Grave."

Cash's voice is at once urgent and hopeful, reflecting the defiant stance of the song's lyrics. Critic Mike Ladano (2013) characterizes Cash's vocal timbre succinctly in his album review, observing that "Johnny's voice is weak, yet that baritone is still so defiantly powerful. Even in illness, Johnny refused to stop making music, his aching voice a shadow of what it once was. Yet even that aching voice stirs powerful emotions through the music." Clearly weathered and worn, Cash's voice in this recording is at times reduced to a pained quasi-whisper, particularly in Chorus 1 (0:08–0:18) and Verse 2 (0:57–1:07). Even his baritone chest voice, most prominent in the latter stanzas of the first and second choruses, sounds strained to the point of breathlessness. However, whereas in some instances these qualities might be seen as detrimental to the final vocal track, here they imbue Cash's performance with rawness and depth that complement the overall lyrical and musical aesthetic. With a lack of studio trickery, Cash's deteriorating voice here suggests honesty and transparency in the performance, traits that contribute to the affective framing of "Ain't No Grave," perceptions of its sincerity, and the recording's unique construction of musical intimacy.

Dimension II: Lyrics

The lyrics to "Ain't No Grave" can be read as an allusion to the resurrection of Jesus Christ, and the Christian belief that after death, followers of Christ will enjoy an eternal afterlife in Heaven. The lyrics are thus celebratory in their defiance of earthly death. Cash's established musical persona (see Chapter 6) of the rebellious outsider reinforces the headstrong attitude in the lyrics, made all the more poignant by Cash's knowledge of his failing health, declining energy, and limited time left to record the project.

While the Cash/Rubin recording makes slight lyrical alterations from those published and recorded by Ely, these are minor, and generally keep with the spirit of Ely's composition. It is also likely that given the many recorded versions of the song, as well as its widespread performance in worship services, Cash may not have relied solely on Ely's version as a reference point. As in Ely's original, Cash sings from a first-person perspective. This is supplemented by second-person modes of address to the undefined "you," as well as direct addresses to the archangel Gabriel, Jesus, and "mother and father," the latter in a stanza that does not appear in Ely's original lyrics. Heard through the context of Cash's final days, this direct address to Gabriel, Jesus, and the subject's presumably deceased parents, along with the broader first-person positioning are unambiguous, and lend the lyrics an affecting, confessional quality, despite not being penned by Cash.

Due to its prominent placement in the mix, it is not difficult for the listener to focus on Cash's vocal delivery and the lyrics. Throughout, Cash alters the phrasing of the lines to bring emphasis to singular words. For example, the first stanza in the chorus, "There ain't no grave," is sung in a rhythm of essentially straight eighth notes, where "there" is anticipated and "ain't no grave" is closer to being metronomically precise (see Figure 2).

Cash alters the vocal delivery with his cadence in the second line, "Can hold my body down," by deviating even more from the essentially straight eighth note delivery of the first line and delaying "body" to the next eighth note (see Figure 3).

By extending the note and giving space to "my" before "body," the musically intimate impact of that line carries added resonance and weight as a result of

Figure 2 "Ain't No Grave" Vocal Rhythm #1.

Figure 3 "Ain't No Grave" Vocal Rhythm #2.

the unexpected phrasing due to the rhythmic manipulation. In addition, a bit of word-painting concludes this line: as Cash finishes the chorus with "down," his pitch and vocal inflection also shift downward to reflect the lyric.

As with the recording overall, Rubin's vocal production is sparse. There is very little musical, frequency, or production overlap when Cash is singing. The production effects and flourishes that are present serve to reinforce a particular line or word in the lyric by employing several more instances of word-painting. For example, in Verse 1 (0:32–0:36), the word "river" at the end of the first line is immediately followed by a wavy, almost wah-wah-like guitar sound, panned just to the right of Cash's vocal. Word-painting continues most notably in Chorus 2, specifically at the end of the second and fourth lines. In each case as we hear the word "down," an acoustic guitar extends the line with a sustained chord (0:47–0:50, 0:53–0:56). In the final chorus (2:21–2:38), the accent on "down" is further embellished with a single tubular bell, suggesting a death knell.

"Ain't No Grave" is a powerful statement of defiance in the face of mortality, performed by an artist who was experiencing a similar situation at the time of recording. This recording's musical intimacy is further enhanced by its construction and form. The subject matter, coupled with the stark musical arrangement and plaintive, borderline confessional vocal, provides a compelling insight into Cash's mental and physical state to the listener, and thus potential perceptions of deep musical intimacy.

Dimension III: Song Construction and Form

At just under two minutes and fifty-three seconds, "Ain't No Grave" is the shortest song on *American VI*. This is another point of contrast between the Cash and Ely recordings. Ely's verses, for example, run for twelve lines, while

Cash's run for a concise four lines per verse. This shortened structure in the Cash version could be a product of the artist's diminished stamina. Although studio technology exists that allows vocal comping and overdubbing to construct the final vocal track under such circumstances, it is a demanding process and most likely would not have succeeded in this case. Vocal comping (building a final vocal track from multiple takes) requires consistency in phrasing and tuning from the singer from take to take, as well as the ability to perform for extended periods of time. At this point in Cash's life, he was not physically able to perform the vocals in this way, and in any case, vocal comping would have gone against the musical and aesthetic philosophy that framed the collaboration between Rubin and Cash. The decision to forego vocal comping, along with the lyrical subject matter, enhances the resonance and power of the shortened structure, as well as the recording process that values immediacy and captures the raw intimacy of Cash's final vocal and instrumental performances.

Other deviations of form in "Ain't No Grave" are instrumental in nature. For example, there is limited dynamic contrast among the instrumental and vocal elements; the instruments are performed and mixed at a relatively consistent, unchanging level. That is not to say that the instrumental elements, particularly the slide guitar, acoustic guitar, and banjo, are devoid of any dynamic variations. Though subtle, these variations can be heard in the fingerpicking, the sustain and decay of the organ playing, and vocal inflections that rise and fall with phrasing and emotional intent.

Another production element that increases apparent dynamic contrast is muting. Muting occurs when a mix element appears in Verses 1 and 2, for example, but then is not heard, or muted, in Verse 3. This element occurs in "Ain't No Grave" most readily with the chains that are played on beats one and three of each measure. The chains enter at 0:21, immediately after the two-bar extension in the middle of Chorus 1. The chains continue the consistent pattern of beats "one" and "three" until Verse 3 (1:45–1:57) and Verse 4 (2:10–2:21), where they are silent. (The chains briefly return for the chorus in between these verses, at 1:57–2:10.) Although Cash's voice is at the same dynamic level in Verses 3 and 4 as it had been previously, the exclusion, or muting, of an element we have come to expect in the verse has a two-pronged effect on the overall mix. First, since the instrumentation is less dense, there is a resulting space in the mix and the apparent loudness of Cash's voice is increased. Secondly, the removal of the chains further exposes the frailty of Cash's intimate vocal performance.

Coupled with its forward placement in the mix, the muting of the percussive chains also lays bare the emotional weight of the lyrics at an especially poignant moment. While the preceding verses anticipate death with some sense of distance, the lyrics in Verses 3 and 4 emphasize its imminence. In contrast, Verse 3 finds the singer ready to meet Jesus, while Verse 4 has him ready to meet his (presumably deceased) parents.[8] Muting the chains over these verses directs attention toward the affectively weighty lyrics, while also allowing Cash's voice to "float" in the mix without the rhythmic anchoring of the percussive chains. In these final verses then, the song structure, voice, and lyrics are all interrelated in constructing a particular moment of musical intimacy in service of the song's overall affective framework.

Dimension IV: Spatiality

The austere instrumentation in "Ain't No Grave" is directly tied to the spatial relationships within and among each instrument, and contributes to a low musical density in the recording. The minimalist production style is a direct callback to 1994's *American Recordings*, and much of the work Cash and Rubin produced throughout the entire series. Cash (1997: 228–9) notes that he and Rubin explicitly worked toward capturing a "late-and-alone, intimate feeling" in those initial sessions, "the honest, unadulterated essence of Johnny Cash, whatever that is." Although "Ain't No Grave" features comparatively more instrumentation and overdubbing than other tracks on the record, the tone and aesthetic of the recording align with the decade-long *American Recordings* collaboration by continuing to feature Cash in a stark, uncluttered sonic space, while employing minimal overdubs and production effects and techniques.

"Ain't No Grave" features two acoustic guitars, an electric guitar, a banjo, percussive foot stomps and chain rattles, an organ, and Cash's vocal. The mixing and spacing of these elements within the recording produce a low musical density; each instrument in the mix is purposeful in its delivery, and there is no extraneous sonic information, leaving plenty of sonic space for each element to come through the mix. Due to the lack of distraction, the supporting instruments are just that; they are all subservient to Cash's brittle vocal performance. As such, the listener is free to focus on Cash's vocal as the primary emotive vehicle in the mix, which is centered in the stereo image, sans effects, with only the slightest touch of dynamic compression. As discussed earlier, other sonic elements of the track (the chains, the bell) have the effect of accenting Cash's vocal rather than directing attention away from it. This placement and presentation of the vocal track create a naked vulnerability that is at once immediate and intimate, serving to strengthen our connection to the song, the vocalist and his plight, the lyrics, and finally, the musical message and aesthetic.

"Ain't No Grave" is a song with a decades-long history; leading off *American VI: Ain't No Grave*, the title song establishes the overall aesthetic of the album, and the dimensions discussed above reinforce and support the intimate aspects associated with death and reckoning. Understanding the association of the artist, the production, and the lyrics, the interconnectedness of the underlying aspects of musical intimacy serves to reinforce the overall message of the song.

"Fetch the Bolt Cutters"

Fiona Apple (2020)

Background

By the time that Fiona Apple released her fifth LP in April of 2020, the world had been effectively shut down by the coronavirus pandemic for a month. Initially slated for release six months later, the pandemic directly influenced Apple's decision to release the album ahead of schedule (Handler 2020). Although not recorded during the pandemic, the album's themes of confinement, conflict, and desire had an added affective resonance in the socio-cultural context of its release, with many listeners under shelter-in-place orders as medical professionals, health care workers, and politicians struggled to understand and respond to the coronavirus. This is further enhanced by *Fetch the Bolt Cutters* being primarily recorded in Apple's Venice Beach home studio, lending to it many of the qualities of home recording discussed in Chapter 2 and addressed more directly below. The title track is arguably the album's centerpiece, a potent concentration of lyrical and sonic themes that are ripe for analysis in terms of its musical intimacy.

Dimension I: Voice

In this section we focus on Fiona Apple's voice in "Fetch the Bolt Cutters," as it is the primary vocal track. Before narrowing our analysis to Apple's lead vocal however, we address the layering of multiple voices throughout the song. From the first chorus through the duration of the recording, the audible voices multiply in a few ways. First, the chorus introduces a second voice, that of British model Cara Delevingne. Delevingne doubles Apple's sung lines (though the two are not always synchronous) and distinguishes herself by harmonizing and, at Apple's direction, emphasizing her British accent (Handler 2020). Composed of only five lines, the second verse (1:27–1:39) introduces a third voice, an overdubbed vocal from Apple. Although brief, the interplay of Apple's two vocal tracks shifts the listener's attention back and forth between them, an effect heightened by the voices' different positions in the stereo soundfield. This layering (and the fragmenting of our attention that it initiates) is especially evident in the song's outro section, where it contributes to a more comprehensive disorienting sonic tapestry. We discuss the unique sonics of the song's outro in relation to Dimension IV: Spatiality; for now, we turn to the recording's lead vocal track.

In a *Pitchfork* interview promoting the album, Apple discussed how her relationship to her own voice evolved since her career began a quarter century earlier. Whereas early on Apple put pressure on herself to deliver technically proficient and aesthetically "beautiful" vocal performances, "Now I'm not so worried. I have fun with my voice now ... I don't feel like I'm such a great singer, like a beautiful voice, but I feel like I'm good at playing my voice. It's just another instrument now. But it's the best instrument. It makes so many noises" (Pelly 2020b). This playful sonic exploration of the voice rather than a polished performance adhering to norms of "good" or "beautiful" singing is apparent in how Apple applies her voice in "Fetch the Bolt Cutters."

Throughout the recording, Apple's voice slides between speaking and singing, often blurring the distinction between the two.[9] When her voice enters into the mix at 0:10, Apple is delivering her lyrics via a melodic phrasing, but at 0:25, her vocal delivery more closely resembles speech, returning to a melodic line to conclude the stanza at 0:31. The second stanza (0:36–1:01) begins with two melodic lines, but Apple quickly situates her voice in a more spoken mode of delivery for the duration of the verse. This speak-singing style presents the lyrics in an informal, conversational tone. At times, the tone and delivery nearly resemble mumbling as if Apple is talking to herself, an affective style that can suggest these passages as a casual conversation or even an internal monologue.

Across this spectrum of singing and speaking, Apple's vocals in "Fetch the Bolt Cutters" are imperfect relative to modern vocal production standards in popular music. Throughout, her voice audibly cracks and wavers, underscoring the unpolished and at times improvisatory approach to her delivery in the song.

Within the initial lines of the first verse, for example, a close listen evinces a voice crack (0:10–0:12). Similar breaks in the vocal tone can be heard throughout the song (as at 1:04–1:06, 1:11, 1:18, 1:22, and 1:42–1:44). Apple has said that while recording this album, she often did not have vocal parts established prior to pressing "record," but instead would take a somewhat improvisatory approach to her vocals, telling *Vulture*, "It's all just unguided … It's very spontaneous" (Handler 2020). This looseness of approach is a luxury not often provided in large format recording studios, where due to time constraints and other pressures, such spontaneity risks jeopardizing the financial risks of studio time.

The intimacy of Apple's style of vocal delivery in "Fetch the Bolt Cutters" is further demonstrated by the many instances throughout the track wherein we hear Apple draw her breath in before delivering a line.[10] Occasionally, this is combined with mouth clicks preceding a vocal line, as at 0:09, 1:39, and 2:46–2:47. Both of these sounds are enhanced through compression of the vocal dynamics in the mix, wherein maintaining a consistent recording volume, quieter on-mic sounds are brought to the fore. Though related to the voice, these non-vocalic sounds evince the materiality of the body, underscoring that the voice is inherently shaped by and inextricable from the singer's physiology (cf. Barthes 1977; Cavararo 2005). In interpersonal interactions, such sounds of breathing and mouth clicks are typically only heard in especially close, intimate encounters. These sonic qualities of Apple's vocal performance in "Fetch the Bolt Cutters," along with the conversational delivery and vocal imperfection, work to establish a sense of performed intimacy, which is especially effective in conjunction with the song's lyrics.

Dimension II: Lyrics

At the denotative level, Apple's lyrics in "Fetch the Bolt Cutters" recount the youthful experience of one-sided friendships, the shame of marginalization and exclusion from a social group, the struggle to assimilate at the cost of personal agency and identity, and the eventual overcoming of that confinement through the actualization and acceptance of self. In addition to the relatability of these common experiences, the sonic qualities of Apple's casual sing-speak style of vocal delivery and the sonics of spatiality reinforce the confessional nature of the lyrics. This is further enhanced by the lyrical framing of the first-person perspective, particularly as heard in Verse 1 (at 0:52–1:02). Throughout the verses, Apple also employs second- and third-person modes of address. Here however, the "you" being addressed is the friend who shamed and refused to accept the narrator ("I was trying to be your friend"). Apple mostly uses the third-person perspective to refer to a collective of "it girls," "PYTs," and "VIPs" who refuse to accept her. It is unclear elsewhere in the song if the third person "you" also addresses this collective or an individual among them. What is clear is that "you" does not directly address the listener; the listener is not hailed as an addressee, but is instead guided to identify with Apple's own subject position.

Without privileging any particular interpretation, journalistic commentary around the album highlighted the sense of relatability and collectivity present in the lyrics of "Fetch the Bolt Cutters." Spencer Kornhaber (2020) suggests in his review that the album's key insight is that "surviving apartness means recognizing it as a shared experience." Although the narrative of the song is framed as personal recollections, Apple validates the shared experience of confinement, while also recognizing that this can take any number of forms within individual experience:

> It's about breaking out of whatever prison you've allowed yourself to live in, whether you built that prison for yourself or whether it was built around you and you just accepted it. ... So I guess the message in the whole record is just: Fetch the fucking bolt cutters and get yourself out of the situation you're in, whatever it is that you don't like. Even if you can't do it physically.
>
> (Handler 2020)

Apple's acknowledgment that such confinement (and desire to break free from it) is defined by individual experience invites listeners to read these lyrics through the lens of their own experiences. For listeners, this relatability can further support perceptions of sincerity in the lyrics, a point to which we return in the conclusion of this analysis.

However one considers the construction of confinement in "Fetch the Bolt Cutters," the subject's intent on escape is clear regardless of the costs, be they social, familial, financial, or otherwise. Although absent in the initial chorus at 1:00–1:25, the second run through this section at 1:40 interjects the phrase "Whatever happens" (repeated once) between the previously established stanzas. The phrase is again incorporated into the final, extended run through the chorus (3:09–4:18), here being repeated a total of ten times. The gradually increasing incorporation of this phrase underscores the call to "fetch the bolt cutters," asserting that the autonomy to be gained from doing so is worth whatever potential costs may come along with this action. This gradual evolution of the lyrical structure is worth studying on its own terms, but within the song's atypical structural form, the evolution gains an added intensity.

Dimension III: Song Construction and Form

As is the case for much of the album, "Fetch the Bolt Cutters" takes a playful approach to song structure, deviating somewhat from standard forms of Western popular music. This playfulness is evident in the song's chordal structure due to not only its dissonance, but also the musicological pun of the song: Apple deliberately arranged the verses to follow a chord progression of C/E—A#maj6—Gm—Em—Dm6, the root notes of which spell out "CAGED," another compositional nod to the song's lyrical themes of confinement (Pelly 2020b).

More specifically looking at the song's structure, "Fetch the Bolt Cutters" follows the common approach in popular music in that the song can be subdivided into eight-bar passages. Within that structure however, Apple arranges discreet sections into unexpected, atypical configurations. For example, a percussion loop provides the core rhythmic track of the song, though this repeating sequence consists of only three bars, each dedicated to a different percussive sound. Heard in isolation at the beginning of the recording, the sequence includes one bar of what sounds like a hand drum, a second bar repeating the same rhythmic phrase on a bright metallic object, and a third bar running straight eighth notes on another metallic object.[11] Mapping this on top of the primary eight-bar structure of the song, the percussion loop and the rest of the song structure do not progress at the same rate; whereas typical structure would find the rhythm sequence beginning with every new four- or eight-bar segment, the beginning of the rhythmic sequence in this recording realigns at the beginning of every thirteenth bar. This creates somewhat of a jagged polyrhythmic orientation, where hearing the first segment of the percussion loop (the hand drum) does not necessarily signal the beginning of a new four- or eight-bar sequence, but instead creates a sonic disorientation where the song's rhythmic structure is not easily discernible.

Similarly, the vocals initiate the first verse (entering at 0:10), though Apple's mellotron accompaniment does not enter for another full bar, whereas typically we might expect it to commence immediately alongside the vocals. Likewise, the song's verses are not uniform in length; the first verse has a thirty-two-bar duration, the second verse has eight, while the third and final verses are spread across forty bars. The song's first two choruses both have a sixteen-bar duration, while the third runs for thirty-two bars before collapsing around the four-minute mark (the track's coda continues for nearly another minute, but is not centered around a common rhythmic structure). These structural alterations are surprising in that they challenge our expectations of typical popular song structure and form. In doing so, the song invites a deeper level of attentive engagement than might be the case for a song that more closely follows established structural conventions. To be clear, it is not that "Fetch the Bolt Cutters" lacks form or structure. Rather, it actively resists conventional standards of popular musical form. This unconventional approach is reflected in other elements of the recording, including its unique sonics and musical density.

Dimension IV: Spatiality

In terms of musical density, "Fetch the Bolt Cutters" incorporates a variety of sounds and instrumentation, but at least initially, does not translate as a particularly dense or busy recording—an aspect underscored by the song's moderate tempo. Journalist Sam Adams (2020) captured this duality well, noting the album's overall sonics are "somehow claustrophobic and roomy at the same time." The song's instrumentation includes vocals (lead, multitracked, and background tracks), mellotron, bass, drums, and a percussion track that features household items such as decorative metal butterfly (Handler 2020). The percussion supplied by these atypical, household items forms the song's rhythmic core, while Amy Aileen Wood performs on the more traditional drum kit. However, the kit does not fully enter the song until its second verse at 1:40. With the other percussion having established the rhythm up to that point (and the relative mixing between the tracks), the drum kit plays more of a complementary role, providing flourishes throughout the third verse, then entering in full for the second chorus and beyond.

The other instruments are quite literally built around the somewhat unusual percussion track. When Apple was inspired to write and record "Fetch the Bolt Cutters," she began only with the song's title and the percussion track, which she had recorded some time earlier (Pelly 2020b). In the final mix, Apple's lead vocal line and the percussion track are the central elements, remaining somewhat static and predictable throughout, and providing a foundation that supports the recording's other layers of instrumentation. The percussion's rhythmic pattern detailed in our discussion of the song's structure goes unchanged throughout the song. Likewise, the mellotron and bass are a constant presence, adding melodic structure and rhythmic shape. Yet both of these instruments are somewhat subdued in the mix, while their initial rhythmic patterns leave a great deal of sonic space. In the first verse for example (0:10–1:01), both the mellotron and bass play predominantly whole notes, setting the tone for each bar, which is then allowed to decay. As the song progresses, both instruments increase their rhythmic complexity, and thus the overall sonic density of the recording. This is most pronounced in Sebastian Steinberg's bass playing which, beginning with the first chorus (1:01–1:26), becomes more rhythmically dynamic and syncopated for the duration of the song while adding rhythmic and tonal counterpoints to the mellotron's chords. As the song culminates in its final chorus and coda section, multiple vocal tracks enter the mix (3:34), adding to the increasing sonic dizziness of this section before it eventually dissipates after the four-minute mark. This progressive development in musical density and movement operates as a kind of tone painting, where the song's gradual build toward a dense, dizzying cacophony reflects the emotional, psychological, and perhaps physical claustrophobia of its lyrics.[12]

One of the defining features of "Fetch the Bolt Cutters" (and the album as a whole) is the spatial context of its creation. Liner notes list both Apple's home studio and Stanley Recordings in Los Angeles as sites of recording and production. Although there is little indication as to the extent of activity that took place at Stanley, the press, promotion, and sonics of the recording suggest that the bulk of recording occurred at Apple's home studio. Throughout the mix of "Fetch the Bolt Cutters," we hear percussion via found objects, inadvertent intimacies, and other indicators that lay bare the trappings of recording in the less controlled domestic environment. Reviewing the album for *Pitchfork*, critic Jenn Pelly (2020a) declared that its sonics "create a wild symphony of the everyday," an apt description well represented by the title track.

Notably, the recording space was not a professionally designed home studio, but a large room converted into something of a makeshift studio, with furniture pushed against the walls, tapestries covering the windows, and little in the way of acoustic diffusors or other means of sound control and absorption (Corcoran 2020). Because of this, a degree of room reverberation is ever present, and is especially audible in the percussion and drum tracks, while the mellotron, vocals, and bass are all relatively dry, as they lack the room reverberation of the percussion and drums. These hints of environmental reverb help to orient listeners to the recording space, which, due to its centrality in the making of the album, became a constant point of discussion in its promotion and press coverage.

A particular inadvertent intimacy also leaves the mark of the domestic space on the final mix of "Fetch the Bolt Cutters." At 3:10, a single dog bark is audible, which we hear again at 3:23. As the song continues through the coda section, a group of dogs is audible at 3:54 and continuing for nearly a minute, adding to the increased density of the song's concluding section (3:10–3:14; 3:23–3:24; 3:54–4:48). In an interview with *Vulture*, Apple explained that Cara Delevingne brought her dogs along to the session, "And so all of our dogs—Maddie [Zelda Hallman's dog], Mercy, Leo, and Alfie—were in this room with the door closed and they're totally silent for the whole take of the song. And then at the end of the song they erupted. It was so perfect" (Handler 2020). Not being intentionally miked, these serendipitous barks reverberate in much the same way as the drums and percussion, as they might in the listener's own home. Recalling our discussion of inadvertent intimacies in Chapter 1, the presence of these barks could have been minimized within the mix by an early fadeout for example, or recording a completely new take. Yet there was a conscious decision to leave them in the final track. We cannot speak to the intent behind this decision, but within the entire sonic palette of "Fetch the Bolt Cutters," the prominence of this canine interruption underscores the sonics and unpredictability of this particular home recording environment.

Cumulatively, these sonic elements of natural room reverberation, the unorthodox use of household objects as percussion, and the inadvertent intimacy of dog barks evoke not only the site of "Fetch the Bolt Cutters" recording, but also the site of the domestic environment more generally. The reinforcement of this setting through reviews, interviews with Apple, and other discourse surrounding the album's release speaks to a twofold intimate spatiality. First, the recording clearly bears the markings of Apple's home and draws listeners into that space. Yet the sonic spatiality of Apple's home can potentially also resonate with the listener's own, a resonance that can be especially strong in the context of pandemic-induced lockdowns, shelter-in-place orders, and social isolation.

Reading "Fetch the Bolt Cutters" through the above four dimensions makes clear the particular examples of musical intimacy in each. The overall aesthetics of the recording have a kind of rawness to them, from Apple's unvarnished, conversational vocal tone to the seemingly uncontrolled sonic spatiality of the domestic recording space. This raw aesthetic in turn plays into notions of sincerity, to the extent that because the recording shuns conventions of technical perfection in performance and production, its expressive qualities can thus be perceived as more authentically sincere. To reiterate a point from the previous chapter however, it is *perceived* rather than actual sincerity that is most important in the context of popular music. While artists, musicians, producers, and engineers can (and do) make deliberate choices to achieve particular effects and affects, their success in doing so is dependent on how the listener receives, processes, and interprets their work. The critical and popular reception for *Fetch the Bolt Cutters* suggests that its musically intimate qualities generally had such affective resonance, an outcome perhaps enhanced by the context of widespread social isolation when it was initially released.

Conclusion

The recordings analyzed in this chapter are by no means the only exemplars of our four dimensions of musical intimacy. The framework that we presented in Chapter 3 is intended to be generally applicable to popular music recordings. That is not to suggest that musical intimacy is constructed or engaged in a uniform way, however. In strategically selecting "Blue 7," "How Come U Don't Call Me Anymore," "Ain't No Grave," and "Fetch the Bolt Cutters" for our analysis, we underscore that musical intimacy is manifest across axes of artist, genre, and time period.

These first four chapters have been centrally concerned with musical intimacy as it is constructed and perceived in recordings of popular music. As we have noted throughout, this is at times deliberate on the part of artists, producers, songwriters, and engineers, but musical intimacy still relies heavily on listener's interpretation and perception. Even if they are often consumed and experienced individually however, recordings of popular music are part of broader networks of commerce, culture, and technology. Importantly, these networks allow not only for the circulation of recordings, but also for the affect associated with musical experience, and its further circulation among audiences' structures of feeling (Williams 1965). With this in mind, in the next chapter we step away from purely sonic concerns to consider other ways in which listeners may be guided or primed for musical intimacy, namely how notions of intimacy are marketed in the popular music marketplace.

Part III

Additional Contexts

5

Marketing Musical Intimacy

Thus far, we have stressed that whatever the intentions of composers, engineers, musicians, and producers, musical intimacy often relies on the interpretive work of audience members, and thus entails a degree of subjectivity on the part of the individual listener. Yet there are a number of ways that artists, as well as labels, and other commercial entities market and promote various forms of musical intimacy, both explicitly and implicitly.

Take for example pianist Teddy Wilson's 1956 LP *Intimate Listening*. The cover photo features a monochrome image of an expressionless woman curled up and seated, seemingly alone wearing her nightgown, yet her face fully made up. The back of the LP's jacket hypes the album by stating that "there is, in the piano playing of Teddy Wilson, a quality of calm directness; it is as though he is playing not for a crowd, not for a recording microphone, not for anyone except the solitary listener." A companion album released that same year continued this emphasis; the jacket copy of the *For Quiet Lovers* LP similarly stresses Wilson's unique playing style, as well as its suitability as a sonic backdrop for romance.

Another notable example is MTV's popular *Unplugged* series. Premiering in 1989, the program continues in various iterations as of this writing, but reached its peak of popularity in the 1990s, when it was a regular feature on the network. The premise of the show brought popular artists into a studio setting to play stripped down, acoustic versions of their material in front of a small studio audience. The marketing of *Unplugged* traded on these performances as a unique experience, advertising the show as a "raw," "up close and intimate" experience for audiences ('MTV Unplugged," "MTV Best of Unplugged Week"), evoking spaces such as small clubs and coffee shops where intimate acoustic performances often occur. NPR's ongoing *Tiny Desk Concerts* video series takes

---

An earlier version of this chapter was published as "'We Are a Fly on the Wall Listening': Constructions of Musical Intimacy in The Beatles' *Anthology*." (2020). *Interdisciplinary Literary Studies* 22.1–22.2: 142–59. This new version is printed with the gracious permission of *ILS* Editors James M. Decker and Kenneth Womack.

a similar tack, inviting artists to play in the cramped office space of *All Things Considered* host Bob Boilen. With minimal amplification and miking, the shoots typically utilize consumer-grade digital cameras and unedited, single takes. Collectively, the sonic, spatial, and visual elements of the *Tiny Desk Concerts* actively strive for and promote the series according to what journalist Zachary Crockett (2016) describes as its "crusade for authenticity."

As with the recent popularity of listening rooms discussed in the next chapter, the frequent promotion of musical intimacy in various contexts suggests its marketability. In addition to the examples discussed above, the growing catalog of archival releases from established artists provides an especially rich area for analysis, and it is here that we focus our attention in this chapter. These releases come in a variety of forms, from single disc reissues, double disc expanded editions, to often lavish muti-disc deluxe boxed sets. A common feature among them is a seemingly bottomless well of previously unreleased material including studio outtakes, home demo recordings, work tapes in progress, and alternate versions. These recordings give fans a glimpse of a particular song or album's evolution and construction as well as capturing the in-studio ambience of the recording sessions. In addition, much of this material can offer a particular form of musical intimacy, presenting often unvarnished recordings of artists in the midst of their creative process, imbued with a documentarian character. As a central object of analysis, this chapter examines The Beatles' *Anthology* albums. Archival releases characteristically present a unique intersection of music fandom and nostalgia, of which *Anthology* is a particularly rich example. Taken together, these frameworks of fandom and nostalgia offer a lens of understanding musical intimacy as a salient characteristic in the popular music marketplace for segments of popular music consumers.

Fandom as Framework

Discourses of fandom are essential to our discussion of archival releases, as it is dedicated fans (as opposed to casual listeners) whom labels and artists court through such releases. However, because it can be engaged, manifested, and practiced in a wide variety of ways, defining fandom is a difficult task. Mark Duffett (2013: 13; 2014a: 7) argues that fundamentally, a fan is someone who has deep conviction about and affective engagement with a famous person or property, and whose identity is to some degree "wrapped up with the pleasures connected to popular culture." The distinction between dedicated fans and other audience members is not always clear, however, as passionate, dedicated fans are also part of a larger, general audience (Cavicchi 1998: 87). Graphically, we might represent this dynamic as concentric circles wherein all fans are members of the audience, but not all audience members are fans. There are layers of inclusion and exclusion at play, with fans having the most intense attachment to a persona, property, or text.

Duffett likens this divide to the concept of a "knowing field" that excludes non-fans. For Duffett (2014b: 154–5, emphasis in original), entering the knowing field means that fans access a particular affective terrain "where one's experience of something strong and positive seems highly personal and yet *more than individual*, since it has a direction and intensity that is shared [by] many others." While much of fandom might be experienced at an individual level, we cohabit in the affective field with others who have invested in the same objects of fandom. The knowing field is where fan communities develop, to the exclusion of non-fans.

Importantly for this chapter, heightened levels of fan interest and engagement often yield higher sales potential as well. Noting their purchasing power, Cavicchi (1998: 62) suggests that fans are the "ideal consumer," given their willingness to buy into a broad array of merchandising associated with the object of their fandom, often tied into the fan's impulse to collect (see also Jenkins 2003). Illustrating this point, archival releases and deluxe editions cater to dedicated fans over new or casual listeners, banking on the purchasing power of a preexisting, affectively engaged fan base. A casual listener is not likely to invest the time or money into a ten-disc commemorative boxed set of U2's *Achtung Baby*, a five-disc expansion of Tina Turner's *Foreign Affair* LP, or a twenty-disc deluxe edition of Metallica's eponymous 1991 album, for example. In contrast, a devoted fan might purchase releases that they already own simply to acquire demos and outtakes not available elsewhere—"double-dipping" in the collector's parlance.

Collecting and curating are among the most common ways that fans engage the object of their fandom. Geraghty (2018: 213–15) argues that "to be a collector is to be a fan," a practice tied up in considerations of capital, gatekeeping, and hierarchy within fan communities. Collectability is often central to the appeal of deluxe boxed sets, the marketing of which emphasizes the physical object and limited production runs. While much of the audio content of these sets may be available for streaming and digital purchase, artists and labels often give great attention to the design and materiality of the physical releases, packing high-priced sets with glossy coffee table books, replicas of relevant ephemera, and unique memorabilia.

The 2018 "Locked n' Loaded" edition of Guns N' Roses *Appetite for Destruction* provides an illustrative example. Limited to a production run of 10,000 copies, the set retails for US$500, and comes in a simulated wood and leather box featuring hand-crafted artwork. In addition to a remastered CD version of the 1987 LP, the set includes three additional CDs featuring forty-nine unreleased recordings, a high-fidelity Blu-ray edition of the album, a ninety-six-page hardcover book, seven twelve-inch vinyl discs, six replica vinyl singles, a USB drive (crafted to emulate the album's cover), eighteen illustrated lithographs, two posters, replica ticket stubs and show flyers, and over forty additional pieces of memorabilia, including rings, pins, buttons, guitar picks, temporary tattoos, a turntable slipmat, and a replica banner. Although this is a somewhat extreme example, it does highlight archival releases' emphasis on the materiality and collectability of the physical release. This emphasis invites a particular engagement between listeners and recorded works, one that simply is not replicated in streaming experience (Alleyne 2022: 6).

For the fan, collecting can be intricately tied up in matters of personal history and identity. Drawing on Pearce's (1995) discussion of fan collecting as an "object autobiography," Geraghty (2018: 219) argues that for fans, collecting is a means to simultaneously narrate the histories of both the object and the fan, and this contributes to the value fans place on objects and texts. This interweaving of personal and material history points to the role that nostalgia plays in fandom and collecting, which further helps to understand how archival releases trade on particular notions of musical intimacy.

Popular Music and Nostalgia

With roots in psychology, nostalgia emerges in a number of contexts, but at its core concerns a longing for a place or especially time "that no longer exists or has never existed" (Boym 2001: xiii–xv). In a landmark study, Svetlana Boym (2001) outlines typologies of restorative and reflective nostalgia, the latter of which applies to our focus in this chapter. Reflective nostalgia is a more meditative, personal mode that is not concerned with attempts to fully recover and reconstruct personal or collective experiences, but instead acknowledges the past's irretrievability, and finds satisfaction in its reminiscence (Boym 2001: 41–9).

Segments of the media marketplace explicitly trade on reflective nostalgia as a mode of consumption; this is perhaps most evident in the rash of remakes and reboots in film and television in recent years, the seemingly limitless extension of film franchises such as *Star Wars* and the Marvel Cinematic Universe, and certainly through anniversary editions and reissues of popular music. The internet has also afforded unprecedented access to media of the past, as well as means to sustain engagement with fan communities centered around these properties. This glut of nostalgically oriented media leads Grainge (2002: 51) to suggest that "the commodification of nostalgia perhaps more accurately demonstrates the contingencies of niche marketing than any particular index of cultural longing."

The marketing and framing of deluxe reissues and archival releases operate through a nostalgic lens, tapping into earlier eras of popular music history and the mythos surrounding particular artists and their work, alongside the audience's personal, historical, and affective relationships with them. Beyond the material dimension of these releases discussed earlier, the music itself is replete with nostalgic potential. At the individual level, music often carries strong relation to personal memories and emotions, with research suggesting that popular music is an especially rich vehicle for all three (Barret et al. 2010; Belfi et al. 2015; van Dijk 2006; Janata et al. 2007). Beyond personal experience and memory, music and other artifacts can also yield what John Koenig (2021: 167–8) terms anemoia, or "nostalgia for a time you've never known." Hence, young adults in the early 2000s can embrace 1960s mod culture and fashion, or two decades later, members of Gen Z can nostalgically immerse themselves in the media and popular culture of the 1980s (Feldman 2009; Reese 2022). Nostalgia does not need to be tied to a time or place one actually experienced.

Nor is reflective nostalgia by any means a link to a "true" past (Boym 2001: xxii; 351–4; Smith 2010: 218). Rather, nostalgia only allows us to engage with the past as it is constructed in the present. In Frederic Jameson's (1991: 19–20) terms, nostalgic media provide only a kind of "pastness," a representation of the past characterized by its "pseudohistorical depth, in which the history of aesthetic styles displaces 'real' history." Complicating this further, nostalgic experiences and objects can work to reshape personal and collective memory, or more bluntly, how "nostalgia [can] become memory" (Wilson 2013: 42). Archival releases, for example, provide a means to access elements of the past, but are also curations presenting a particular, fixed version of that past. In the process, there is ample opportunity for selective memory and historical revisionism in a way that can serve to reinforce or reshape the historiography and mythology surrounding particular artists and albums; such releases are thus not simply documents of popular music's past, but the present's engagement with (and potential rewriting of) it.[1] That is, nostalgia presents not a documentation of the past, but an ideological narrative (Stewart 1993: 23), a "false archive" (Leising 2018), or a "sentimental myth" (Jenkins 2003: 157). The Beatles' *Anthology* collections provide a case in point. They are false archives on account of their editing and curation, which entailed conscious choices regarding what to release and what to exclude, and how to construct a particular version of The Beatles' mythology. Central in the *Anthology*'s presentation of this mythology are the constructions of musical intimacy featured throughout the project.

The Beatles' *Anthology*: A Case Study in Constructing Musical Intimacy

In 1995, the surviving Beatles rolled out the *Anthology*: a sprawling multimedia endeavor documenting the history of the band and its celebrated discography. Initiating with a three-part television broadcast, the *Anthology* also included a ten-hour home video set, a large-format book, and an audio component, released as three double-disc sets between 1995 and 1996. The *Anthology* set includes 147 musical selections, among them unreleased tracks, live performances, alternate versions, and the first "new" Beatles songs in a quarter century, the refurbished Lennon demos "Free as a Bird" and "Real Love."

The project also vividly illustrates how archival releases serve not only to provide insight into an artist's work, but to simultaneously reinforce their pop cultural mythos. Critic Steven Hyden argues that part of what allows the concept of "classic rock" to maintain cultural currency is the mythology surrounding its artists. Hyden refers not simply to fabled tales of rock star excess and sexual conquest, but the many ways that the legendary status of classic rock's most enduring artists is perpetuated well after their periods of peak commercial activity. The canonization of certain catalogs, the creation and tenacity of oldies and classic rock radio formats, the production of biopics and documentaries, and the commemoration of milestone anniversaries through reissue campaigns, reunions, and concert tours all serve to maintain the vitality of classic rock mythologies (Hyden 2018; Reynolds 2011).

More specifically to The Beatles, the group's mythology had a quarter century of circulation and refinement between their 1970 breakup and the release of the *Anthology* project in 1995. The temporal distance between the *Anthology*'s release and The Beatles' breakup arguably makes the project not only more salient in terms of a market demand for new product, but also more impactful as an artifact, further enriching and sustaining the group's mythology, which is in part accomplished through the musical intimacy presented across its six discs. In the case of The Beatles' *Anthology*, musical intimacy manifests via aesthetic minimalism, sonic access to private spaces, and the aural voyeurism of hearing The Beatles working through their creative processes. We note, however, that these are not rigid demarcations, as selections from the *Anthology* often exhibit characteristics of multiple categories. Nor do we suggest that other archival releases demonstrate musical intimacy in exactly the same way. However, The Beatles' *Anthology* albums provide a template for how archival releases can construct, frame, and market musical intimacy to fans eager for new material.

Aesthetic Minimalism

As we discussed in Chapters 3 and 4, spatiality is a common aesthetic that can connote intimacy, especially when a recording has a particularly sparse arrangement. In contrast to recordings with dense layers of multitracked sounds, sparse or minimalist arrangements draw attention to what aural components are present in the recording as there is simply less aural data for listeners to process. Exemplary here are seven tracks included on *Anthology 3* that originate from a May 1968 demo session at George Harrison's home in Esher. These private, informal sessions served as preliminary recordings in preparation for what became *The White Album*. While some of the Esher recordings included on *Anthology 3* feature minor flourishes such as double-tracked vocals and light percussion ("Mean Mr. Mustard," "Polythene Pam," "Glass Onion," "Piggies," "Honey Pie"), others are essentially solo acoustic performances ("Happiness Is a Warm Gun," "Junk"). The minimalist arrangements in these recordings connote intimacy in part because of the associations that solo, acoustic performances carry within rock culture, as noted in the introduction to this chapter.

Moreover, the minimalist arrangements in the *Anthology* recordings provide a heightened contrast to the more dense and polished productions of their officially released versions. The *Anthology 3* version of "All Things Must Pass" recorded at Abbey Road features only Harrison and his electric guitar, with a second, overdubbed guitar part. The eventual release of this song on Harrison's 1970 album of the same name is by contrast a rather dense arrangement, characteristic of the album's producer Phil Spector. The 1970 recording features two guitars, an additional pedal steel guitar, an electric bass guitar, two drummers, and a piano, as well as string and horn arrangements (Leng 2003; Whitlock 2011). Likewise, the Harrison composition "Something" appears on *Anthology 3* as a solo demo recorded in early 1969, again featuring only Harrison's vocal and guitar. As it appeared on the *Abbey Road* LP later that year however, "Something" features Harrison's double-tracked vocal, guitar, bass, a second guitar, drums, organ, and a lush, twenty-one-piece string arrangement (MacDonald 1994: 278).

Such aesthetic disparities between the established, released versions of these songs and their *Anthology* counterparts serve as a means of facilitating listener engagement. Perceived musical intimacy and the concept of listener engagement are intertwined, and in many instances, the overall sonic impact of the track is a result of the musical forces interacting in ways that reinforce, extend, and maintain a space of musical intimacy where the listener may remain engaged.

The novel appeal of these alternate configurations is dependent upon familiarity with the officially released versions that by 1995–6 were entrenched in popular culture through consistent radio airplay and sales performance spanning three decades. This cultural prominence in turn forces a level of mental engagement from audiences as they listen, actively comparing these newly released early takes with their well-known canonic counterparts. Even in songs such as "Octopus's Garden" where there are no drastic differences between the *Anthology 3* and previously released versions, listening to the early takes included on the *Anthology* provides illumination and insight into the creative process of the song's evolution. Thus, while the *Anthology* facilitates musical intimacy at the aesthetic level via minimalism, it also fosters a different, more personal kind of musical intimacy, via active listener engagement with multiple versions of the tracks when listeners are familiar with the canonic version. Yet as with many archival releases, the sense of musical intimacy on the *Anthology* albums is doubly emphasized when listeners are granted sonic access to the private spaces where The Beatles wrote and recorded.

Sonic Access to Private Spaces

Over the years, bootlegs of The Beatles' recording sessions proliferated among collectors, while Mark Lewisohn's (2004) exhaustive research provided extensive documentation and insight into the band's studio activity. However, for the overwhelming majority of audiences, exposure to and familiarity with the group's work was limited to the authorized, officially released canon. The studio recordings presented on the *Anthology* albums offer an expanded view of this body of work, albeit one that is meticulously curated. Especially important here is the role of various sites of significance within The Beatles' well-known biography, including those in Liverpool (The Cavern Club, The Beatles' childhood homes), Hamburg (The Kaiserkeller, The Indra Club), and London (EMI's Abbey Road Studios, the Apple Building). These spaces are central in The Beatles' artistic and professional development, and are inseparable from their biographical narrative.

The *Anthology* albums grant listeners sonic access to a number of such biographical spaces, peeling back the veneer of the group's officially released material. The recordings do so not simply by virtue of providing a fixed, aural document, but by the evocation of particular parallel spaces in the listener's mind, which in turn lends a perception of aural voyeurism or "witnessing" of the music's creation (see Hagood 2019: 117). Although popular music recordings are deliberately mediated constructions, listeners engage something akin to suspension of disbelief, or what Brovig-Hanssen (2013) discusses as "transparent mediation"—the listener's willingness to ignore the mediated, constructed nature of the sonic performance (17). As Walther-Hansen (2015: 33; see also Auslander 2008; Marshall 2003) notes, this willingness is part of what allows listeners of popular music "to engage in an imagined relationship with the performer, by participating in a perceived performance event."

Many of the *Anthology* recordings foster such relationships by granting sonic access to intimate spaces throughout the group's evolution from Liverpudlian teenagers in the late 1950s to seasoned professionals crafting their swansong in 1969. The first archival recordings on *Anthology 1* take us to Phillips Sound Recording Service in Liverpool, a crude, makeshift living room studio where the group (as The Quarry Men) cut two sides in 1958 (Lewisohn 1995: 6–7). These are followed by a trio of songs recorded by the newly christened Beatles in 1960, committed to reel-to-reel tape in Paul McCartney's childhood home in Liverpool. The *Anthology* albums continue this approach even through The Beatles' years of professional recording and international stardom. *Anthology 2*'s second disc opens with a solo demo of "Strawberry Fields Forever," recorded by Lennon at his home in Weybridge, Surrey, in mid-November 1966 (Lewisohn 1996a: 29–30). *Anthology 3* likewise invites listeners to George Harrison's home in Esher, where The Beatles made the aforementioned demo recordings for *The White Album*. Recalling our discussion of home recording in Chapter 2, the intimacy of the above series of recordings is further enhanced by their framing as private, home recordings, bearing the sonic markers of crude, amateur recording techniques and decades of tape degradation: room sound, tape hiss, and an overall low fidelity recording. Although not up to contemporary consumers' standards, the flaws inherent in the recordings mark them as sonic artifacts of popular music history, that, alongside their framing as private home recordings, facilitates the perception of intimacy. Yet as regards sonic access to private spaces, the bulk of material on the *Anthology* takes listeners inside perhaps the most mythologized site in The Beatles narrative, EMI's famed Abbey Road Studios in London.

Although some artists now utilize social media and streaming sites to publicly document the process of musical creation (see, for example, various "studio diaries" on YouTube), studio recording and production have historically been a private activity, shielded from public view. In part due to the mystique of this activity, a kind of mythology develops alongside some of the more renowned studios, to the extent that they become tourist attractions for music fans. Among these mythologized sites of artistic creation are preserved studio spaces of Fame Studios in Muscle Shoals, Alabama, Motown's Hitsville USA in Detroit, Sun Records and the reconstructed Stax Records in Memphis, and Prince's Paisley Park studio complex in Minneapolis. Yet perhaps no recording facility has been mythologized to the same extent as London's Abbey Road studio.

As The Beatles' primary workspace between 1962 and 1970 (and immortalized in their 1969 album of the same name), Abbey Road is imbued with its own cultural mystique. As Bennett (2016: 397) observes, Abbey Road has become "part shrine, part tourist attraction and part heritage site for those interested in The Beatles and general popular music history." Along with other Beatle locales such as The Cavern Club, Penny Lane, and Strawberry Field, Abbey Road is exemplary of what Crowther and Steinberg discuss as a "living archive," places and environments in which a subject lived that go on to inform their work, and which in turn have a particular allure for fans and researchers seeking a deeper understanding of both the artist and their art. In other words, a living archive "exists as history on the ground. A place, a house, or even a room can contain an archive because it houses time, events, memories, and past histories. Places tell stories too" (Crowther and Steinberg 2017: 37–8).

It is the shared history of The Beatles and Abbey Road that feeds the mythology of the site, at once increasing its allure and status. To be sure, following The Beatles' success, Abbey Road became a magnet for artists, labels, and producers, yielding landmark productions by Pink Floyd, The Alan Parsons

Project, Radiohead, Lady Gaga, Florence and the Machine, and The 1975, among many others. The commercial success of such recordings continues to amplify Abbey Road Studios as a standard-bearer and destination for sonic excellence, cementing its reputation as a premiere, world-class recording facility. To be sure, the Abbey Road mystique has been one of the facility's selling points for decades, and continues to be so as the studio taps into the booming home recording market.[2] In short, among the many spaces to which the *Anthology* recordings grant listeners sonic access, the Abbey Road Studios hold a unique status given their role within The Beatles' own mythology.

Aural Voyeurism

The musical intimacy of the *Anthology*'s Abbey Road recordings plays out in two significant ways. First, it invites listeners to bear aural witness to The Beatles' creative process in the studio—learning material, working through song structures, experimenting with arrangements, and breaking down mid-take. On *Anthology*'s first volume, a sequence of excerpts from a March 1963 session finds The Beatles struggling to get through "One after 909." McCartney falls out of Take 3, complaining that without a pick, "it's murder, I can't do it, can't keep it up," while Take 4 breaks down following Lennon's early vocal entry. Later on *Anthology 1*, Lennon also struggles with vocals in an early take of "I'll Be Back" from June 1964, complaining that "it's too hard to sing, when I start going 'oh oh' about eight times." Take 1 of "Yesterday" from *Anthology 2* provides an especially clear example. Recorded on June 14, 1965, this initial work-through begins with tentative strumming from McCartney as Harrison inquires of the song's key. Demonstrating the chord progression as he replies, McCartney relays that "It'll be in F for you I'm in G but it'll be in F. It goes E minor to A7 to B minor." This first take of "Yesterday" presents musical intimacy by offering a glimpse into the formative stages of a Beatles classic, and through the intimate aesthetics of its delicate solo-acoustic arrangement.

Secondly, by virtue of transparent mediation and granting sonic access to the private space of Abbey Road Studios, the *Anthology* also grants access to intimate moments within the group's interpersonal dynamics. Removed from their calculated celebrity personae and the spotlight of Beatlemania, these informal interpersonal interactions illuminate the camaraderie within the group, and as aural witnesses, recall the listeners' perceived sense of participation discussed by Walther-Hansen (2015).

Two takes of "No Reply" included on *Anthology 1* are demonstrative in this regard as a flub of the lyrics yields humorous confusion. As the second verse concludes in Take 1, Paul transposes lyrics from an earlier verse; whereas Lennon's lead sings a line that ends in "I saw you walk in / Your door," Paul's backing vocal mistakenly sings "face" in place of "door." Whether intentionally or by accident, Lennon interchanges two further lyrics in the take, yielding laughter from himself and Paul. In Take 2, Lennon correctly completes the line, though he does so through audible laughter, perhaps recalling the inversions from the earlier take. A series of takes of "Eight Days a Week" (also from *Anthology 1*) presents a similar mood of laughter and frivolity. A single track edits together three false starts of the song, each of which quickly breaks down with laughter and playful insults from Paul.

Also notable in this regard is *Anthology 2*'s vocal overdub of "And Your Bird Can Sing," recorded on April 20, 1966. Musically, the take closely resembles the familiar version issued on the *Revolver* LP later that year. However, what begins as an earnest vocal attempt quickly finds Lennon and McCartney erupting in hysterics and struggling to regain composure, ultimately resorting to whistling through the song's coda. In similar fashion, a work-through of "Oh! Darling" on *Anthology 3* is interrupted by a phone call alerting Lennon that Yoko Ono's divorce from Tony Cox had gone through; the band briefly resumes the tune, improvising new lyrics to celebrate the occasion (3:25–4:00). Moments such as these poke holes in the façade of the polished perfection of their previously released iterations. In addition, they serve to humanize The Beatles, fostering a sense of intimacy that may otherwise be absent from the personae crafted and maintained by their status as pop cultural icons and musical legends. Collectively, these takes of "No Reply," "Eight Days a Week," "And Your Bird Can Sing," and "Oh! Darling" express a fluidity in the studio, providing sonic evidence of the band's enthusiasm for the songs and for the process of their refinement through purposeful rehearsing. Moreover, this shared spirit of camaraderie and playfulness allows listeners to witness the group's dynamics during the process of creation, though as we discuss below, hostile or unflattering interactions are notably absent.

Across six discs, the *Anthology* albums present musical intimacy in a variety of ways: through aesthetic minimalism, granting sonic access to private spaces, revealing The Beatles' creative process, and inviting listeners and fans to actively engage with the material. Importantly, however, we must recognize that these are not raw historical documents, but commercial products produced for a worldwide, record-buying fan base. As with the book and video components of the project, the *Anthology* albums are meticulously curated constructions; at times they intentionally exploit technologies of production in part to foster a sense of musical intimacy, but also to present an aural document that serves to reinforce The Beatles' well-established mythology.

Constructing Musical Intimacy

Although Harrison, McCartney, and Starr were heavily involved in the *Anthology* albums, the construction of musical intimacy therein was largely achieved through the editorial directives of producer George Martin. At a press conference tied to the release of *Anthology 1*, Martin described the project's intent to present The Beatles "in the raw, it's warts and all. Got mistakes there, and you've got funny little things happening. But it's honest, and it's what we did. And you hear, you hear us talking, you hear the boys commenting, you hear them breaking down and so on. We are a fly on the wall listening to The Beatles" ("The Beatles—Anthology I Press Conference"). Martin's claim about the nature of these released recordings does not quite reflect the reality of what the *Anthology* albums present to listeners, however. While some tracks were edited for time, others were edited into composites of multiple takes—including those whose titles are parenthetically marked "complete" in the track listings. One obvious composite is the version of "Yes It Is" included on *Anthology 2*. This track begins with the sparse second take, which breaks down one minute in. As it does so, the track conspicuously crossfades into Take 14, which boasts a fuller mix, slower tempo, and more polished production aesthetic. In fact, Take 14 became the master for the B-side released in 1965. This blatant edit simultaneously underscores and undermines the intimacy of Take 2 by contrast, and remains a rather odd editorial decision on the part of George Martin.

The remaining fifteen composite mixes on the Anthology successfully mask the edit points, giving the perception that they are each single, continuous takes. To be fair, these alterations and splices are not exactly well-guarded secrets; Mark Lewisohn's liner notes for the *Anthology* albums provide transparency in detailing session dates, takes, and alterations made for this release. Even so, we can only speculate as to George Martin's intentions, though the effect of this editorialization is twofold. First, some of Martin's decision-making is in service of fostering a perception of musical intimacy with listeners. Given the heavy editing across the *Anthology* for time and content, it is somewhat odd that we get so much studio banter, joking around, and talking through the process of piecing these songs together. These moments of candor could certainly have been edited out, but Martin made the conscious decision to leave them in the mix, ostensibly to facilitate an intimate aural experience by putting listeners into the studio space with the Fab Four, making them privy to the group's creative process. Moreover, the inclusion of all of these aural elements on the *Anthology* allows Martin and the band to construct a narrative and biographical element to this archival release, presented as an historical sonic document.

Secondly, these editorial decisions undermine Martin's characterization of the *Anthology* set as "raw," instead reasserting his initial aim to present The Beatles "as best I possibly could" ("The Beatles—Anthology I Press Conference"). In that sense, the *Anthology* albums serve to supplement and reinforce the band's mythology—their artistry, their workmanship, and their interpersonal dynamics—rather than demystifying it. These observations underscore that to some degree, the musical intimacy presented on the *Anthology* albums is an active construction by Martin, the production team, and the surviving Beatles. For interested listeners and fans, however, the *Anthology* albums provide an historical, though heavily curated document—one that through exploitations of musical intimacy offers new perspective and insight into The Beatles' catalog. To that end, the constructed pastness that the *Anthology* and other archival releases present to listeners stands to become the new referent, standing in for previous releases; nostalgia, in effect, becomes memory (Wilson 2013).

Conclusion

Archival releases have proliferated since the release of the *Anthology* series in 1995–6, and they have taken many forms. Within The Beatles' constellation, these include deluxe anniversary editions of *Revolver* (2022), *Sgt. Pepper's Lonely Hearts Club Band* (2017), *The White Album* (2018), *Abbey Road* (2019), and *Let it Be* (2021), as well as ongoing reissue campaigns from the solo catalogs of Harrison, Lennon, and McCartney. Aside from repackaged and expanded editions, another strain of archival boxed sets chronicle the recording sessions of a given album (e.g., The Beach Boys' *The Pet Sounds Sessions* (1997); The Stooges' *The Complete Fun House Sessions* (1999); Miles Davis' *The Complete On the Corner Sessions* (2007)) or time period (e.g., Johnny Hodges' *The Complete Verve Small Sessions 1956–1961* (2011); Ahmad Jamal's *The Complete*

Trio Argo Sessions 1956-62 (2010); Paul Robeson's *Complete EMI Sessions 1928-1939* (2008)). On a smaller scale, it is also now commonplace for greatest hits collections and career retrospectives to include archival material alongside previously issued recordings (e.g., Michael Jackson's *The Ultimate Collection* (2004); Dolly Parton's *Dolly* (2009); Tom Petty's *An American Treasure* (2018)). Despite the many variations of how popular artists' archival work is packaged and marketed, there are commonalities throughout.

First, previously issued works containing unreleased archival material are directly aimed at dedicated fans rather than a general audience. As discussed earlier in this chapter, collecting is primarily a fan practice. Archival releases directly appeal to fans' interest in collecting, in terms of both an emphasis on physical releases (via limited editions, custom packaging, and the inclusion of memorabilia), and the desire for completism. Promotion of archival releases sometimes directly addresses this impulse, as in an advertisement for The Beatles' *Anthology 1* that proclaims, "You haven't heard everything yet" ("Beatles Anthology Ad 1995").

Second, archival releases present an avenue for reflective nostalgia, connecting listeners' present with a personal and historical past, weaving an intricate matrix of personal and cultural memory. Central to this particular nostalgic construction is not the past itself, but rather a deliberate *pastness* (Jameson 1991). By their very nature, archival releases such as boxed sets and deluxe editions construct pastness as they represent, recontextualize, and reconstruct albums, catalogs, and artistic legacies (Alleyne 2022). Bottomley (2016) notes that this reframing occurs through extra- and paratextual material in archival releases (extensive liner notes, hype stickers, semantic framing of "deluxe," "ultimate," and "definitive" editions) as much as through the supplement of previously unissued recordings.

This inherent, constructed pastness highlights the third characteristic function of archival releases: they provide opportunity to revise, reframe, and enhance the mythology of the artist or work in question. In some cases, the mythology is part of the attraction, as in The Beach Boys *Smile Sessions* set, released in 2011. Shelved after tumultuous recording sessions in the 1960s, the *Smile* tapes were heavily bootlegged and circulated widely among collectors and fans in the ensuing decades. The 2011 set presents a configuration of the storied album, alongside five discs' worth of "outtakes, sessions, and studio banter" ("The Beach Boys SMiLE," 2011). Framed by liner notes extolling Brian Wilson as a creative genius, these intimate recordings bolster the mythos of Wilson's arranging and compositional skills, in turn folding back into *Smile* as a project of stature and importance within The Beach Boys' oeuvre, and the broader rock canon. That is, for archival projects such as The Beatles *Anthology* or The Beach Boys *Smile Sessions*, intimacy becomes a major point of marketing as it grants listeners access to informal, hitherto private material. Instead of demystifying the work or the artist, however, these particular iterations of musical intimacy serve to further enhance the artist's mythology and the work's canonization. Yet, the deliberate curation of such false archives does not necessarily refute the legitimacy of audiences' sense of musical intimacy, emotional investment, or affective engagement. Even so, as listeners we have to remain conscious of the fact that such releases tend to be histories selectively told—acts of self-curation and preservation of cultural legacies that arguably exploit as well as foster musical intimacy among listeners.

6

Intimacy and Live Performance

Up to this point, our primary concern has been how musical intimacy is constructed, manifested, and perceived in recordings of popular music. In this chapter, however, we shift focus to consider live performance across three different contexts. Our first area of examination is musical performance in physically intimate spaces, where the proxemics of such a performance engender a sense of intimacy by their very nature. Yet musical intimacy in popular music performance is not limited to the confines of listening rooms, coffee shops, and small clubs. As such, we examine two further performance situations, both of which would seem to preclude opportunities for musically intimate experiences. The first of these is intimacy within the spectacle of popular music performances in large-scale venues such as arenas and stadiums; the second is the profusion of online livestreams and video performances that quickly emerged amid the Covid-19 pandemic. We analyze these various iterations to understand how musicians are able to cultivate a sense of musical intimacy and connection with audiences through live performance. In doing so, we pay particular attention to how aesthetics, affect, and parasocial relationships can be manipulated to engender a sense of musical intimacy, even when matters of scale, scope, and technological mediation present obstacles to such experiences.

As with all of its forms more generally, musical intimacy in performance is at root a matter of relationality between artists and audiences, and certainly within audiences as well. The types of relationality apparent across the performance contexts that we examine are fundamentally different than those of popular music recordings discussed in previous chapters.

In the case of performances in intimate spaces, this primarily concerns the close physical proximity between artist and audience, encouraging a more direct sense of engagement than may be possible in larger-scale venues or electronically mediated performances. On the other hand, musical intimacy in the context of large-scale concert performances and those in digital spaces are inherently marked by distance and technological mediation. We argue that in those cases, the sustained cultivation of musical personae and parasocial relationships is a major factor in the construction of and engagement with musical intimacy.

Intimate Spaces, Intimate Performances

Musical performances of any scale are to some degree governed by the spaces that they inhabit. Be it a midsize club, a large stadium, or a private house party, each involves its own characteristic use of space in terms of size and arrangement, as well as how a particular space promotes or inhibits behaviors, movements, and interactions. With that in mind, proxemics provides a means for considering spatial dynamics of such musical performance. Initially developed by Edward T. Hall (1963, 1969), proxemics deals with how we organize and utilize space, from micro-level concerns such as room arrangements and workspace layouts to larger-scale matters including the zoning and organization of buildings, roadways, and public space.

As an anthropologist, Hall's primary concern was how proxemics and culture influence one another in terms of behavior and social norms. Additionally, proxemics provides an insightful framework for how we might understand the role that varying spatial dynamics have in shaping intimacy in live musical performances. Yet even here, "intimacy" is a fairly subjective notion, with wide variation how the term is applied. For example, Madonna's 2019 *Madame X* tour was billed as "an intimate concert experience," booking theater venues with capacities typically around 3,000. Conversely, a tour of the same venues by an unsigned act that typically plays a small club with a 200-person capacity would likely not be considered "intimate." Still, the theaters booked on the *Madame X* tour are certainly intimate in comparison to the 15,000 seat arenas where Madonna typically performs. In some ways then, intimacy in performance is a matter of relative scale, as well as one of branding, marketing, and the musical persona of the performer.

In smaller venues, such as mid-sized clubs with capacities in the hundreds, or listening rooms where the maximum capacity ranges from twenty to fifty members, space becomes more intimate not only between the performer and the audience, but especially among audience members. The smaller the venue, the greater its sociopetal orientation (Hall 1963: 1008; see also Osmond 1957).

That is, smaller venues necessarily pull people into closer physical relations that in other social contexts might be considered a violation of personal space.

Here, sensory dimensions work in tandem to define both the space and the activities that it hosts. In discussing "intimate distance," Hall (1969: 116) argues that "the presence of the other person is unmistakable and may at times be overwhelming because of the greatly stepped-up sensory inputs. Sight (often distorted), olfaction, heat from the other person's body, sound, smell, and feel of the breath all combine to signal unmistakable involvement with the body." At a DIY "house show" for example (see Verbuč 2017; Verbuč 2018), a crowd of listeners might pack into a residential basement for a local punk band's performance. Here, intimate proxemics become defined not just aurally (by the music, the cheers and applause from appreciative listeners, audience members shouting over the music in conversation) and visually (the minimal distance between audience and artist, even less between audience members), but also through olfaction (the musk of sweat and body odor, hints of intermingling deodorants and perfumes), tactility (the audience standing shoulder to shoulder, the inevitable bumping and pressing of bodies, catching drops of others' perspiration on your own skin), and thermics (feeling the body heat radiating from those around you). This may not be the kind of sensory experience listeners would seek out independent of such performances, but in context, they temporarily endure, and in some cases even embrace such "sticky intimacy," as it contributes to an "affective intimate community" across the physical and social dimensions of DIY ethos (Verbuč 2017: 293–4). Moreover, such close quarters allow for both spectatorial and co-creational listening (Verbuč 2018), while also giving rise to affective transmission between participants, who may well be exchanging such information through perspiration, olfaction, and pheremonal activity (Brennan 2004). A raucous basement punk show provides an extreme example of intimate proxemics, particularly in relation to the sensory dimensions outlined by Hall. Even so, performances in other types of small spaces similarly lend themselves to a unique matrix of intimacy between artists, audiences, and music, as is the case with increasingly popular listening rooms.

The designation of "listening room" can refer to a diverse array of venues. In some cases, these are existing establishments such as art galleries, church halls, and coffee shops that occasionally repurpose their space in order to host musical performances. Among the most unique of these, for example, is The Salt Sanctuary in Wheeling, West Virginia: a Himalayan Salt Therapy room that occasionally hosts live music. Often, however, listening rooms are dedicated commercial spaces that emphasize intimate performances for audiences intent on focused listening and increased opportunity for interaction with the artist. To that end, many self-described listening rooms have stated policies barring conversation and cell phone use during performances. Just outside of Pittsburgh, Pennsylvania, for example, Steamworks Creative (Vento n.d.) asks its patrons to refrain from talking, to remain seated, and to silence cell phones during performances. The Roasting Room (n.d.) in Bluffton, South Carolina makes a similar stipulation in its policies, also noting that in the case of excessive talkers, staff will "politely ask you to finish your conversation on the porch outside and return with a quieter disposition out of respect for the artist and those around you." Although these are specific examples, such policies are common across self-identified listening rooms in the United States, an effort to cultivate a controlled performance and listening environment.

Through their promotional framing, listening rooms emphasize the intimacy that audiences can experience at their venue.[1] For example, The Bugle Boy (n.d.) in LaGrange, Texas declares that its "Listening Room environment creates the best and most intimate experience that an artist can share with an attentive audience." The Velvet Note (n.d.) in Alpharetta, Georgia boasts on its website that at the venue, "you will always enjoy the feel of the intimate, private concert and up-close-and-personal conversation you've dreamed of having since you first discovered the artist's talent." 20 Front Street (n.d.) in Lake Orion, Michigan describes itself as a "Mostly acoustic, intimate listening room designed to evoke sound quality and provide a live music experience unlike any other venue in our area." This promotion of "up-close-and-personal," intimate musical performance is a virtue of the proxemics afforded by such venues.

Taking capacity as a metric for such intimacy, a brief review of listening rooms in the United States shows great variance in this regard.[2] Capacity can run anywhere from twenty-five to thirty-five people on the lower end (such as at The Salt Sanctuary in Wheeling, West Virginia and The Sandbox in Kalamazoo, Michigan) up to 200 persons (as at The Armory in Fort Collins, Colorado and The Bloom Café and Listening Room in Bristol, Tennessee), and even up to 350 patrons (as in a standing room only setup at The Square Room in Knoxville, Tennessee).

These widely divergent capacities underscore that even in considering what is arguably one of the most apparent presumptions of intimacy (physical proximity with others and small group settings), intimacy is an inherently subjective term, in large part because it is a matter of perception, be it emotional, relational, spatial, or sensual. Moreover, while small venues designated and marketed as listening rooms are a somewhat recent phenomenon, functionally they are nothing new; similar venues have of course been a part of the performance ecosystem for much longer. Small public spaces such as coffee houses, community centers, and galleries have historically hosted musical performances, while many small clubs and bars have capacities comparable to the larger listening rooms. What makes listening rooms distinct from these other spaces is that they explicitly trade on the concept of a musically intimate experience.

The self-appointed distinction of listening room operates to rhetorically differentiate these performance spaces, even if they are functionally similar to other small venues. This suggests that as with the multimedia recordings discussed in the previous chapter, intimacy is a valuable, and thus marketable quality in live musical performance. The proxemics of a 30-seat listening room and a 10,000-seat amphitheater offer qualitatively different musical experiences. Still, even larger venues are often able to make overtures to perceptions of intimacy between artist and audience, a unique manifestation of musical intimacy to which we now turn.

Intimacy within the Mass

By virtue of their size and scale, large concert venues such as amphitheaters, arenas, and stadiums would seem to work against any sense of intimacy between artist and audience, instead being more prone to facilitating intimate dynamics between audience members. Despite the physical distance between artist and audience at such venues, many performers attempt to foster audience perceptions of intimacy through the personae that they enact on stage.

By persona (pluralized as *personae*), we simply mean the totality of an artist's publicly accessible identity. The concept of celebrity persona is multifaceted, and has received extensive treatment in scholarship on film, media, and performance (e.g., du Preez and Lombard 2014; Graver 1997; Horton and Wohl 1956; Marshall 2016; Nowell 2012; Scott 1991; Smith 2014; Valentinsson 2018). Bringing this notion of persona into the arena of popular musical performance, musical personae are uniquely complex, and fundamentally different from those of film, television, and theater. When we watch actors and actresses on film, stage, and screen, we are able to differentiate that performance as a role temporarily enacted by the individual. This delineation tends to be much murkier in relation to musical performance, where personae are "constructed for the specific purpose of playing music under particular circumstances … What musicians perform first and foremost is not music, but their own identities as musicians, their musical personae" (Auslander 2006: 102–3).

Auslander (2021: 86) goes on to emphasize that musical personae are co-constructed and negotiated between artist and audience, as meaning is made at the site of consumption and perception. This positioning underscores the audience's investment in an artist's musical persona, which in turn builds their expectations to see a particular persona enacted when attending a concert performance, for example. Moreover, audience investment in and expectations of musical personae can be problematic for artists, who may grow to feel stifled by the limitations of their persona. In some cases, the artist's musical personae overshadows the music itself; the braggadocious online musings of Kanye West or the flamboyant dress and personality of Rick James come to mind here. In addition, while there is surely no guarantee that audiences will follow, musical personae can change and evolve over time. In the case of David Bowie for example, the continual shifting of characters (e.g., Ziggy Stardust, Aladdin Sane, Halloween Jack, The Thin White Duke, et al.) became an attraction in and of itself, contributing to a broader persona of Bowie as a chameleon in terms of both persona and musical style.

Increasingly, this collaborative construction and maintenance of musical personae is sustained through social media and related digital platforms. Nancy Baym suggests that this connectivity requires a rethinking of audiences and personae. Baym (in Baym, Cavicchi, and Coates 2018: 149) offers the notion of "false intimacy" as replacement for parasocial interaction, as the former "allows for the possibility that the relationship is in fact social, not 'para,' but that one person feels a much closer bond than the other."

Elsewhere, Baym (2018: 19–20) understands this as a growing source of relational labor that demands an increasing amount of time and skill, sometimes at the cost of relational boundaries. This relational labor creates a sense of connection between artists and fans, particularly in terms of "getting to know" the artist; fans may perceive artists' social media presence as granting access to latter's backstage behavior, even if in reality it is simply another deliberately curated facet of their front stage presentation (cf Goffman 1959). More importantly, however, artists' ongoing relational labor operates in service of their musical personae, an increasingly multi-platform endeavor that also includes recordings, live performances, publicity photos, music videos, press interviews, and fan discourse.

Persona, person, and personality are related, but not interchangeable entities. When as fans we engage with the artist's crafted, curated persona, we typically do not gain access to the person or their personality. The persona may well reflect the person, but this is not necessarily so (Auslander 2006: 103). Artists vary in their level of attention in constructing their persona, and some may avoid any conscious effort to do so. Especially elaborate musical personae seemingly emphasize artifice, highlighting the theatricality of performance, as is the case with Lady Gaga, David Bowie, and Sun Ra, for example. In contrast, the "commonfolk" personae of artists such as Jason Isbell, Bill Withers, or Joni Mitchell may connote a greater sense of authenticity in their seeming lack of spectacle; yet this does not mean that they lack a musical persona, nor that their identity is not itself carefully constructed. In all cases, it is the fan's perception of the musical persona and its outward performance that matters, regardless of the artist's level of investment in its construction.

As mediations (Meintjes 2003: 8, 260–1), musical personae are "both a conduit and a filter" for the artist's music and its performance, each shaping and reinforcing the other while also serving as an intermediary between artist and audience. Because musical personae are co-constructed with audiences, fans have an invested stake in that personae's engagement and maintenance. This symbiotic relationship in turn shapes not only audience expectations as noted above, but also the relationality between the musician and the individual audience member, even if there is no tangible, direct interpersonal interaction. The mediating role of musical personae makes perceptions of musical intimacy possible in the context of a concert performance in front of thousands of spectators, a phenomenon Steven Connor (1997: 174) refers to as "manufactured mass closeness," a performance style that Bruce Springsteen has perfected over the course of his career.

In Concert: The Intimacy of Bruce Springsteen

Bruce Springsteen provides an especially vivid example of how one's musical persona can work to create a sense of musical intimacy while playing to large audiences. Across a catalog that currently spans over twenty studio albums (to say nothing of his cadre of secondary material in the form of B-sides, live recordings, archival releases, and retrospective compilations), sixty music videos, and a consistent cycle of concert tours, Springsteen has amassed a significant body of work through which he has shaped and reshaped his musical persona.

This persona has not been exactly static over the decades, but neither have its mutations been especially jarring or in conflict.

Throughout his career, academic and popular literature has consistently commented on the perceived authenticity of Springsteen's musical persona (Bird 1994; Cavicchi 1998; Frith 1988; Grossberg 1988, 1989; Sheinbaum 2010, 2020), particularly by way of his "everydayness" (Woge 2007), his stance as a "common citizen" (Wolff 2014), his projection of (and appeal to) working-class identity (Cowie and Bohem 2016; Hemphill and Smith 1990; Petkovski 2010; Pfeil 1993; Stephens 2018), and his seeming lack of artifice in composition and performance (Frith 2013: 240). This projection of an authentic, working-class persona is especially effective in the case of Springsteen, as it is coupled with lyrics that operate within an affective system that articulates the pleasures and pressures of the working class while simultaneously highlighting the ordinariness of these experiences, "a lyric form suited to a more intimate style" (Grossberg 1988; Rauch 1988: 30).

Fronting the E Street Band, Springsteen early on earned a reputation as an exceptional live performer, with energetic concerts that regularly clocked in between three to four hours in length—a work ethic that further shaped and reinforced his musical persona. As success gradually took him from small clubs to large arenas and stadiums by the mid-1980s, the physical intimacy of smaller venues was naturally inhibited by the sheer scale of concerts regularly attended by tens of thousands of spectators. Yet in making this transition, Springsteen adopted a performance style and stage presence that sought to exploit the dynamics of such large audiences rather than falter at the limitations therein.

Consider Springsteen's penchant for storytelling in concert. During extended introductions or breakdowns of certain songs, Springsteen would often tell stories reflecting his working-class upbringing, his tense relationship with his father, the evolution of his political beliefs, and of the mythology of the E Street Band. These exceptionally detailed and descriptive stories serve as another means of establishing and maintaining an affective dynamic with his audience, who may be able to see themselves in the "everydayness" of Springsteen's on-stage storytelling. As Frith (2013: 240) argues, whether or not Springsteen's lyrics and stories come from lived experience matters far less than their affective power and subsequent role in connecting with audiences.

Fans and critics often liken Springsteen's mode of address in live performance to that of a revivalist preacher, an aspect of his persona that has intensified over the years (Beach 2018; Duncan 1978; Robb-Dover 2012; Randall 2011;

Toppman 2014). Although Springsteen's personal religious beliefs are somewhat ambiguous, Beach (2018: 69, 83–4; see also Masciotra 2010) points out that faith still figures centrally in Springsteen's music, his rhetoric, and performance; in command of the stage and engaged with his audience, Springsteen is "able to take religious ideas and employ them in ways that evoke the power of their meaning but in a way that is accessible and meaningful to his largely secular and politically diverse audience."

This is readily apparent in how Springsteen—as gravelly voiced, fire-and-brimstone preacher—often addresses his audience from the stage. The introduction to performances of "Spirit in the Night" is instructive in this regard. As the E Street Band meditates on an introductory, organ-drenched minor E chord, Springsteen often howls from his rock and roll pulpit, "can you feel the spirit?" His audience-cum-congregation cheers in response, and the exchange often goes on to incorporate both Springsteen's brand of rock and roll sermonizing as well as antiphonal exchange with the audience. Springsteen similarly adopts pastoral language in metadiscourse about the relationship between his band and the audience, as in his proclamation that "We're here to serve you," made throughout the E Street Band's reunion tour in 2000 (Beach 2018: 74; Carlin 2012: 400).

This role of the preacher-showman employs a kind of "communal framing," demonstrating "the respect and reciprocity between Springsteen and his audience as Springsteen frames the concert as a journey shared by the audience, the artist, and the band" (Esposito and Raymond 2018: 95). More precisely, Springsteen's stage performance (as shaped by and engaging with his musical persona) generates what scholars have alternately described as *communitas* (Turner 1969; Turner 1974), "light touch gatherings" (Thrift 2005), and "liquidarity" (Garcia 2011): spontaneous, loosely organized, affect-rich formations that generate a temporary sense of solidarity among a group of strangers that otherwise lacks any other form of concrete, social cohesion. Despite their heterogeneous makeup, such formations are ripe for generating intimacy among members, however fleeting they may be. Luis-Manuel Garcia (2011) for example, demonstrates how crowded dance floors establish such loose social formations, and give rise to an ephemeral, but profound intimacy between strangers. Edith Turner (2012: 43, 48) argues that music's ephemerality strengthens rather than diminishes its ability to generate such temporary unity, as well as its ability to unite people in space and time. This is the manner of intimate social relation that Springsteen generates in performance, even in a 20,000+ seat arena such as Madison Square

Garden. Whether he beckons the audience to take over singing the first verse of "Hungry Heart," to strum his guitar during encores of "Born to Run," allowing audience signs to dictate portions of the setlist, or seeking affirmation that they can, in fact, "feel the spirit," Springsteen in concert orchestrates not only his musicians on stage, but the crowd's engagement with the music that they are playing.

At the same time however, discourse on Springsteen emphasizes the feeling of this connection also being individualized. Here too, Springsteen's musical persona of an authentic, American everyman plays a part. But in Springsteen's case, establishing a sense of individual connection with audience members also relies upon the sentimentality of his performance, music, and lyrics. Grossberg (1988) argues that this "over-indulgence of the affective" is part of what accounts for Springsteen's popularity. For Grossberg (1988: 59),

> sentimentality defines a discursive realm within which we get to live out affective relations which exceed our lives and always will; it not only places affect above meaning, but places intensity—the quality and quantity of affect—above specificity, as if it were necessary to feel something more intensely than is available to us. There is a *democracy* of affect which can only be traversed by an ever-spiralling search for an excessive affect necessarily divorced from the contingencies of everyday life.
>
> (emphasis in original)

Along with his musical persona, this emphasis on sentimentality facilitates a sense of direct connection between Springsteen and individual audience members. The perceived authenticity of his everyman musical persona in turn supports the authenticity of sentimentality in his performance.

While both the musical persona and sentimentality are present in Springsteen's recorded work, they are even more pronounced in his live performances, and this may in fact be part of what makes so many of Springsteen's audience members repeat attenders. In his qualitative study of Springsteen fans, Cavicchi (1998: 55) notes that "having a personal relationship with Springsteen means that one feels deeply about Springsteen the performer ... fans are not so much touched by Springsteen himself as by his performance." This sense of personal connection appears frequently in popular discourse about Springsteen's performance style. Jon Garelick (2019), for example, argues that Springsteen's brand of "'audience engagement' felt like a personal connection to each of us in the crowd. It was big, and grand, and full-hearted, but it was also intimate." Writing for *Forbes*, Bruce

Weinstein (2018) raised the question directly: "How can someone playing to thousands of people make each person feel so special?" Eventual bandmate and wife Patti Scialfa told director Thom Zimny (2010), "The first time I saw Bruce was in 1978. I'd never seen anything like that. It was shocking. I was surprised that you could be in such a large venue and still feel that you're having a personal experience." A fan similarly relayed to San Jose journalist David Kerns in 2012, "I felt astounded that I could feel that way when I'm with thousands of people. It felt like he was talking to me."

Baym (2018: 20) highlights a central tension for artists engaged in relational labor, wherein artists "must simultaneously manage the relational demands of each person who reaches them and play to the crowd as a whole, with all of the diverse audiences of allies, antagonists, strangers, and others it contains." Here, Baym is speaking of music audiences in broad terms, not strictly those related to live performance. However, the tension she articulates encapsulates the seeming contradictions in navigating a concert performance to an audience of thousands, while also seeking to make a personal connection. As the case of Bruce Springsteen illustrates, successfully negotiating this tension is achievable not simply through sheer musical talent onstage, but through the ongoing labor of cultivating, maintaining, and realigning one's musical persona, while also leveraging an excess of affect by way of sentimentality. From 2020 through 2021, Springsteen produced a bi-weekly radio show for Sirius XM, *From My Home to Yours*. Through the intimate medium of radio, Springsteen presents musical selections along with his own ruminations on life, music, and current events. At a time when live performance was effectively suspended in light of the Covid-19 pandemic, the radio program allowed Springsteen to continue to engage his musical persona while connecting with fans, albeit in a manner that is highly mediated. With such limited/non-existent opportunities for live performance, many musicians took to the internet during the pandemic, crafting new ways of enacting musically intimate experiences with listeners; the next section explores this phenomenon in greater depth.

Intimate Performances during Covid-19

In 2020, the worldwide Covid-19 pandemic sent the live music and entertainment industries into an economic and artistic tailspin. Most support personnel were sidelined as well, with global industry losses of nearly $30 billion for the 2020 calendar year (Aswad 2020). Live venues shuttered indefinitely, while many municipalities issued lockdown or shelter-in-place orders, severely limiting face-to-face social interaction. Coupled with the sense of social isolation, the absence of live music within this landscape created a void not only in performance, but also in terms of connection between fans, artists, and their music.

Artists quickly took to the internet and social media platforms in an attempt to fill that void, maintaining a connection with fans through posting video content to streaming platforms such as Facebook, YouTube, and Instagram, often live and simultaneously distributed across multiple platforms. This transition in live performances from physically to virtually shared spaces also forced a reconsideration of the parameters of liveness beyond notions of a performance context that emphasize simultaneous co-presence, and out of necessity embracing mediatized performance (Auslander 2012). Couldry (2004: 356) suggests the category of "online liveness," characterized by a real-time co-presence in a shared virtual space. While this can be an inherently interactive space such as a live chatroom, it can also refer to a broader audience consuming the same online content, akin to a traditional imagined community (cf. Anderson 1983). Auslander (2012: 6) further suggests that "the emerging definition of liveness may be built primarily around the audience's affective experience." That is, the user experience "feels live," even if it is mediated through an audio-visual stream, or perhaps even if it is recorded and consumed asynchronously. With musicians' Covid-era video content, this affective dimension to digitally mediated liveness is enhanced by appeals to parasocial interaction.

In this context, parasocial interaction exploits the aesthetic, technological, and presentational qualities of mass media to "give the illusion of a face-to-face relationship with the performer" (Horton and Wohl 1956: 215). Horton and Wohl's (1956: 216–17) initial work in this area argued that through attention to the studio set, framing of the shot, gestures, language, and tone of voice, television personalities establish "a bond of intimacy" and that "even if it is an imitation and a shadow of what is ordinarily meant by that word, is extremely influential with, and satisfying for, the great numbers who willingly receive it and share in it." In Hartmann and Goldhoorn's (2011: 1107) terms, parasocial relationships are one sided, but cultivate a "felt reciprocity" on the part of the audience.

Caughey (1986: 226, 247) furthers the parasocial argument by pointing out that the fan-artist dynamic is primarily a social relationship, and one that fans perceive as beneficial. To that point, effective parasocial framing can enhance audience receptivity to media content; when media content contains strong parasocial appeals, audiences tend to view the content as being more valuable, more meaningful, and more enjoyable than media content that makes no such attempts at parasociality (Auter and Davis 1991; Hartmann and Klimmt 2005; Herrerra 2017).

Parasocial interactions are thus a means for understanding audience relationships with media figures, and one that has endured throughout a drastic technological evolution in our media systems. While Horton and Wohl's initial formulation considered the unique parasocial dynamics of television, more recent work has established that digital platforms including social media and YouTube afford the cultivation of parasocial relationships in unique ways (e.g., Ballentine and Martin 2005; Chen 2014; Kassing and Sanderson 2009; Kurtin et al. 2018; Rasmussen 2018). Musicians' video and livestream activity during the Covid-19 pandemic provides another opportunity to observe how artists employ particular approaches to audio-visual aesthetics and means of bodily and vocal address to enable parasocial interactions, which in this case we argue also fosters musical intimacy between artists and fans.

It is worth noting that the ease with which these interactions occur in contemporary media contexts is a culmination of decades of immersion in media from traditional broadcast television, radio, print, and increasingly sophisticated media-rich presentations through online media channels. Technologies that strategically implement audio, visual, textual, and interactive components enable and expedite intimate online connections and interactions (Miller 2012: 225). As a result of the viewer's engagement with the content of streaming video for instance, the cumulative effect of discrete parasocial interactions result in the perception and reinforcement of ongoing parasocial relationships that in turn reinforce the viewer's perception of a personal connection to the artist.

A number of livestreams and videos during the pandemic were shot in the apparent home of the artist, presenting a *mise-en-scene* that supports a construction of intimacy from the viewer's perspective. These videos often present a domestic scene adorned by couches, coffee tables, drapery, and comfortable lighting, with artists dressed informally and presented in a medium shot or a more intimate medium close-up; in short, the visual aesthetics of pandemic-era livestreams seemingly invite viewers into artists' homes, just as we digitally welcome them into ours. Here, as in television and film, what Meyrowitz (1986: 262) terms "the framing variable" plays a crucial role, as it "places the viewer within scenes ... Shots portray distances and therefore have a 'meaning' which corresponds to the functioning of spatial cues in interpersonal interaction." The proxemics and intimate setting depicted in the frame ideally serve to establish a similarly intimate sense of connection within viewers.

The modes of bodily and verbal address in those frames are also crucially important in establishing the groundwork for a parasocial interaction. Verbally, musicians in these videos and livestreams tend to adopt a casual, conversational tone, directly addressing viewers in first- (I/we) and second-person (you) language. This individual appeal is typically complemented by the visual, bodily address of breaking the fourth wall, and making direct eye contact with the camera/audience member. Studies of media personae's implementation of these direct modes of verbal and physical address find that they work to humanize the media persona, increase audience engagement and intimacy, and ultimately make media content more personal to the audience (Auter 1992; Auter and Palmgreen 2000; Bennett 2014; Cummins and Cui 2014; Herrera 2017).

In addition to considerations of aesthetics and address, many online video platforms incorporate comment sections and live chat features, where viewers can interact with each other and potentially with the artist. Such features further strengthen parasocial relationships, even if the artist does not respond directly to user messages—simply having the potential for them to see and respond to audience chats has been found to be effective in this regard (Rasmussen 2018).

Collectively, these features—setting and visual appearance, vocal and bodily address, and interactivity—make contemporary video platforms ripe grounds for building and maintaining parasocial interactions with artists, and this was arguably enhanced during the pandemic's prolonged periods of social isolation. Although these Covid-era videos and livestreams tend to share similar aesthetics and approaches, there is some variation among them in terms of the performance context itself. To that end, we have found that these mediated performances tend to fall into one of three main categories: the solo artist communicating one-on-one to the audience, broadcasts of the band playing co-present in the same physical space, and virtual collaborations between bandmates in different spaces. We examine each category in kind below.

One-on-One

One strand of online performances during the pandemic situates a single performer in front of the camera, simulating a one-on-one encounter with viewers. These clips feature musicians playing in their own domiciles, often in a living room or home studio. There is thus a coziness conveyed through the *mise-en-scène* of these clips, while they also provide a kind of parity between the artist's domestic space (as a site of production) and our own (as a site of reception).

In a series of especially demonstrative examples, KISS frontman Paul Stanley uploaded a number of videos to Instagram early on in the pandemic (some of which were later uploaded to the KISS YouTube channel). Though Stanley did not maintain this activity for an extended period, the videos in this small sample vividly illustrate parasocial tactics. Spread across five Instagram posts from March 27 to April 6, 2020, the videos depict Stanley in what appears to be his home studio, or perhaps a makeshift practice space. The setting is open and inviting, with just a few pieces of musical equipment in the shot. The quality of the video and sound is highly professional; Stanley is well lit, with no shadows, and the sound is exceedingly clear. Throughout the videos, he speaks in a calm, conversational tone (as opposed to his characteristically bombastic style of crowd address during concert performances), and employs first- and second-person language, inviting us into this shared virtual encounter. For example, after opening his March 30 post with a solo acoustic performance of 1992's "Every Time I Look at You," Stanley asks the camera,

> Did you miss me? Well honestly I missed you, especially now that I hear that we're gonna be inside at least another month … Here we are again. I'm here, you're there, but we're friends, we're connected. Me playing for you, obviously, it's not a record, it's not gonna be perfect, but if you were at my house, it wouldn't be a record, and it wouldn't be perfect. But that being said, it's awesome to be together.
>
> ("Paul Stanley Sings" 2020)

In a clip that posted on April 6 (but apparently recorded two days prior), Stanley similarly welcomes fans into his domestic performance space:

> How you doing, everybody? Um, I think it's uh, Saturday, April 4th, had dinner and, uh, quite honestly April 4th is just like April 2nd and probably the same as April 6th will be. Um, all days are pretty much the same so uh, (sigh) are we bored? Yeah! Um, I'd like to be able to do more than I'm doing, but it's great to be able to spend some time with you, and uh, just get uh, together … This isn't a performance, it's not a concert, it's not a recital, it's me and you hanging out. And that means that uh, is it perfect? Hell no. But uh, we get to have some fun.
>
> ("Paul Stanley Checks" 2020)

Later in that same video, Stanley invites viewers to participate in the performance from home: "I thought, maybe I'll play some, just some riffs, play some little guitar parts, and ah you can sing if you want, um, you're in the band! If you know the parts of the song, sing along. It's just us. You, me, and I don't know, 200,000 people? 300,000 people?" ('Paul Stanley Checks' 2020). In these introductions, Stanley initially defines the videos by what they are not (records, performances, concerts), and primes users' perceptions of musical intimacy through his rhetorical framing ("I missed you," "It's great to be able to spend some time with you"). Throughout, these videos, the content feels spontaneous rather than scripted, as Stanley sits on a stool with his guitar, sharing stories from his time in KISS, or about the history of a particular song or genre. Presumably, artists like Stanley produce these videos in part to provide a balm for fans during a particularly trying time, when so many viewers are restricted in where they can go, and with whom they can interact. Furthermore, the tone of the videos is one of relaxed conversation and music, helping to transform musically intimate bonds through live performance into ones that are supported, reinforced, and enhanced by streaming technology.

The Paul Stanley videos put many archetypal parasocial techniques on display, though they lack one of the key elements of parasocial interaction. Since Horton and Wohl's initial article in 1956 (and affirmed by studies of more recent platforms, e.g., Rasmussen 2018) the literature has stressed that instances of parasocial interaction with a media persona be regular occurrences, building and reinforcing the broader parasocial relationship over time. DJ and Roots drummer Ahmir "Questlove" Thompson's pandemic livestreams stressed this kind of regularity, at least initially. Beginning on March 22, 2020, Questlove frequently livestreamed DJ sets from his home, simultaneously distributing them through multiple platforms including Instagram Live, YouTube, and Twitter. A stationary camera faced Questlove's DJ station, pair of turntables and a mixer in front of him, a spacious living room behind, often with a fire blazing. The viewer's screen also showed Questlove's digital DJ interface, displaying artists, song titles, bpm rates, runtime, and waveforms of his selections in real time. Throughout 2020, Questlove streamed live DJ sets multiple nights per week, sometimes theming sets around particular artists or styles, often interjecting to share relevant pieces of music history and trivia. Because the sets were presented in real time (as opposed to being prerecorded), users also had the ability to chat during the sets (though not across platforms). Although not an active participant in the chats, Questlove did occasionally respond verbally to chatroom goings on. This added layer of interactivity goes beyond the comments section of pre-recorded posts on YouTube and Instagram, emphasizing the privileged status of online liveness discussed by Auslander (2012) and Couldry (2004). Questlove's DJ sets are not as explicitly parasocial in nature as Stanley's videos; they feature significantly less emphasis on direct eye contact with the camera, and less direct bodily and verbal address. But the visual framing of the domestic space, the relaxed tone, the interactivity of the chat, and Questlove's storytelling still exudes a sense of connection between him and his audience, one that is notably absent from seeing him perform at a large venue or his regular gig on *The Tonight Show Starring Jimmy Fallon*.

The lack of formality and overall relaxed atmosphere of many Covid-era performances often couples with the dual domestic dynamic (the transmission from the artist's home to that of the audience) to emphasize a casual, intimate musical encounter. Vocalist and pianist John Legend ("John Legend", 2020) doubled down on informality in his March 17, 2020 Instagram Live performance. Legend's clip opens with him immediately breaking the fourth wall, fumbling with his phone. Once the phone is steadied and Legend is seated on the piano bench, he confesses, "As promised, I am pantsless, I have a robe on, and no pants. But I do have underwear on, in case you're curious. So what songs do you all wanna hear?" Continuing this emphasis on informality and coziness, Legend's wife Chrissy Teigan joins the broadcast ten minutes in, taking a seat on the piano itself, wearing a robe and head wrap, and drinking a glass of wine. The couple's four-year-old daughter Luna also eventually joins the frame, sitting on the piano and cuddling with her mother. Although Legend is the only person performing music in this clip, the domestic framing (including a collection of his Grammys displayed next to the piano) combines with the visible family interaction to connote a sense of togetherness, comfort, and intimacy throughout.

The Co-present Band

A number of Covid-era videos depict a group of musicians playing together in a shared physical space. An interesting subset of these videos feature musicians and their progeny, or established family acts. For example, following the pandemic-induced cancellation of Willie Nelson's 2020 Luck Reunion festival, the event shifted to a virtual livestream format on March 24th, linking up performers from across the country. Alongside sons Lukas and Micah, Nelson headlined the event from his ranch outside of Austin, Texas, the intended site of the festival. Visually, this performance features stark lighting, and a lone, at times unsteady camera fixed on a tight, immobile shot of the three musicians as they share a bench in the family's living room. The musical arrangement is simply vocals and three acoustic guitars. Neither guitars nor voices are directly miked, lending the audio track plenty of natural reverberation, and giving audiences a sonic orientation to the room in which the Nelsons are performing. That sonic orientation underscores the physical and familial intimacy between these men, as they sing and play together, harmonizing vocals or taking passes at soloing, as when Lukas casually says "take one, dad" during a performance of Lukas' own "Just Outside of Austin" ('Lukas Nelson' 2020).

John Fogerty took a similar approach for a series that debuted on his YouTube channel on April 6. Taking place at various sites throughout the family's property, the clips find Fogerty and his three children, Shane, Tyler, and Kelsey, gathered in a semi-circle, playing renditions of hits from Fogerty's back catalog. Dubbed "Fogerty's Factory," the clips typically feature a mix of unmiked acoustic and amplified electric instruments. Early entrants in the series did not mike vocals directly, again sacrificing fidelity but providing a clear sonic sense of the space. The pre-recorded videos feature Fogerty prefacing a particular song by telling stories about music, childhood, and family, the latter element emphasized in the description for the series' debut clip: "Bringing a little light from our home to yours. We are having a little family fun together during the pandemic. It's such a great feeling to be making and playin' music surrounded by love. We all need to celebrate the life we have and remember how precious it is" ("Down on the Corner" 2020).

Fogerty's description emphasizes the familial component of his YouTube series, and underscores that this strand of videos have an added affective layer within the body of Covid-era performance videos. These representations of family artistry and togetherness came at a time when many families were in social isolation together, and while many other people were unable to physically visit family members in their homes, hospitals, or care facilities. The affective dimension of parasocial interaction in these clips is arguably intensified, emphasizing familial intimacy through a medium of musical performance. The dynamics here may thus be less about an audience member's parasocial relationship with a musical persona, and more tuned to the affective instigation to consider (or identify with) one's own familial relationships during a time when for many, familial dynamics were drastically altered from the norm.

Another family performance is illustrative of a larger trend in media during the pandemic, in which the aesthetics of remotely recorded online performances bled from social media platforms into prime-time entertainment. Doing so effectively normalized what had hitherto been an exception, not a rule in broadcast media. Following an initial period of reruns, late night talk shows began to experiment with teleconferencing platforms and remotely recording content. Hosts including Jimmy Fallon, Trevor Noah, Stephen Colbert, and John Oliver recorded show segments from the safety of their homes, while guest interviews took place over what had quickly become the familiar visual interface Zoom and similar programs.

Musical guests too, often performed remotely. On April 29, *The Late Late Show with James Corden* aired a pre-recorded clip of Green Day's Billie Joe Armstrong along with sons Joey and Jakob performing Tommy James and The Shondells' 1967 hit, "I Think We're Alone Now" ("Billie Joe Armstrong", 2020). Like many of the Covid-era video performances, this clip is somewhat minimalistic in its framing: a well-lit, overhead, single-camera shot in Armstrong's home, with no prefatory or concluding dialogue. The video is tightly edited, and features high-quality audio of the minimalist drums-bass-guitar-vocals arrangement. Taken as a whole, the Armstrong family's performance exudes a personality and a warmth that continues to reinforce and contribute to a strong feeling of musical connection and intimacy between the performers on screen, and between the artist and the audience. Moreover, the song choice of "I Think We're Alone Now" aids the affective intensity of this performance. Perhaps selected as a somewhat tongue-in-cheek commentary on the social isolation of the pandemic, the lyrics' yearning for physical, potentially sexual intimacy underscores the desire for contact amid social isolation.

In similar fashion, *Saturday Night Live* rounded out its forty-fifth season with three weeks of *SNL At Home*, relying on remote and prerecorded content. On the April 23 program, the sole musical segment featured a remotely recorded clip of Miley Cyrus performing Pink Floyd's "Wish You Were Here" (1975), accompanied by guitarist Andrew Watt.[3] The clip is visually warm, the entire frame drenched in a red filter, as Cyrus and Wyatt perform the song around a campfire. These intimate visuals are complemented by the sparse musical arrangement, and like the Armstrong clip, the song selection itself. The lyrics of Pink Floyd's 1975 ballad express a yearning for reconnection, despite harboring "the same old fears," an all too fitting sentiment as audiences dealt with the physical disconnection from friends and loved ones during a public health crisis that we struggled to understand.

Satellite link-ups and other means of remote connection have been part of broadcast media for decades, but the integration of pre-recorded and homemade musical performances into primetime television performed a few functions specific to the context of the pandemic. Most obviously, it contributed toward the ability for these programs to continue producing and distributing content in service of advertisers, audiences, and networks. At a secondary level, however, it normalized this style of content, readjusting both our conception of musical performance, and accordingly our expectations as viewers. This echoes earlier shifts, most notably Auslander's (2008: 56) observation that the designation of "live" performance only has value in opposition to its counterpoint of recorded performance, a distinction brought on with the introduction of sound recording and motion pictures in the twentieth century. Extending this thinking to the context of Covid-era performances, the shift is not solely about a fundamental category of "liveness," but also the extent to which we as viewers are willing to accept new aesthetics, and in some cases, even the illusion of liveness in mediatized performances. The description to Sheryl Crow's April 24, 2020 upload of her 1994 hit "All I Wanna Do" nods to this reconceptualization of liveness: "We miss playing for you, so we are inviting ourselves over to play for you live-ish" ("Sheryl Crow", 2020). The exclamation of "live-ish" is a recognition of (and perhaps resignation to) the transition from a live performance space to an artificially constructed, technically mediated space. Though perhaps made offhand, "live-ish" acknowledges that this is a fundamentally different experience than a traditional concert in a shared space and time. Yet as with earlier semantic compromises such as "live broadcast" and "recorded live," "live-ish" was the best that audiences could hope for within the limited opportunities for live music and connection to artists in the midst of the Covid-19 pandemic (Auslander 2012: 5).

Musicians in Different Spaces: Stitched Performances

When considering Covid-era artists' digital uploads, the most abundant material consists of clips featuring bands playing together, though in different spaces. In these instances, onscreen we typically see each musician in their space simultaneously, separated by the all too familiar demarcations of videoconferencing software. As naturalized as such performance videos became during the pandemic, it is an illusion that subtly asks the viewer to buy in to the façade that the band is playing together in shared time, if not space. However, current bandwidth and technological limitations preclude such real-time performances through the internet due to obstacles of latency, or time-lag. Such lag is less noticeable in the context of a one-on-one Zoom call or a team video conference where speech dominates the audio stream. Musical collaboration, on the other hand, demands shared, synchronous understandings of rhythm, which the inherent latency of the internet makes virtually impossible. Latency in a recording session or performance situation, especially when multiple performers are interacting with one another, hinders the timing and interaction between musicians.

In this set of performance videos, the technological hurdles introduced by latency and compressed audio quality are overcome by copious amounts of editing and post-production. In short, each musician's part is recorded separately, then stitched together to synchronize audio and video tracks between band members, presenting the illusion of a live performance via teleconference. The value of the illusion, of course, is that to the viewer it *seems* live, and thus carries all of the valuations and connotations of liveness discussed throughout this chapter. Even where viewers may be aware of this technological construction of liveness, there is perhaps a willingness to suspend disbelief in the interest of supporting the performance. Furthermore, the construction of this illusion is deliberate and directly supports and strengthens key elements that inform and help to mediate musical intimacy, as if the performers and audience members were in the same space interacting.

Previously, we discussed the normalization of remotely recorded performances through their exhibition on prime-time television. On April 18, 2020, Global Citizen (an arm of the larger Global Poverty Project) produced *One World: Together at Home*, a benefit to raise funds for the World Health Organization's Covid-19 Solidarity Defense Fund. The media event spanned broadcast, cable, and online platforms, and produced eight hours of content. The two-hour broadcast portion gathered a series of musicians, entertainers, and celebrities to perform from their remote locations, while appealing to viewers to contribute to the fund. Some of the performances were artists performing solo while others remotely linked two or more band members simultaneously.

The Rolling Stones served as one of the broadcast's marquee acts, and their performance demonstrates how this platform strives for the illusion of liveness. The Stones' portion of the program begins with a black screen divided into four quadrants, marked "Mick Cam," "Keith Cam," "Ronnie Cam," and "Charlie Cam," respectively. As Mick's cam "goes live," he appears in a domestic space with an acoustic guitar, addressing the audience and breaking the fourth wall: "Here's one I hope you know, and you can join in if you want." He then shifts his gaze from the camera to his left, as if addressing his longtime bandmate and creative partner through the still-blank "Keith Cam" screen, "Everyone ready? Okay." Jagger counts off the song, and proceeds to begin a performance of 1969's "You Can't Always Get What You Want" on his own. As the song and video progress, the remaining band members appear in their quadrant as their respective instruments emerge in the audio mix, with drummer Charlie Watts' entrance preceded by a visual glitch, though it is unclear as to whether this is genuine or added for effect.

In each Stone's "cam," there are no visible mics—suggesting that vocals by Richards and more noticeably, Jagger, are either not directly miked, or done so at a distance ("The Rolling Stones", 2020). As with other examples discussed earlier, this translates to an abundance of room sound, giving viewers a sonic orientation to the space in which Mick is performing, connoting the warmth and reverberation of the domestic space rather than the sonic depth and refinement of a closely miked vocal performance. These details aid in perceptions of musical intimacy in that through the subtle use of acoustics, audiences gain a sonic orientation to Jagger's performance space. Yet, the Stones video also pokes fun at the illusion. When drummer Charlie Watts appears in his quadrant, he is not behind a drumkit, but is instead seated low to the floor, playing his part on a set of small road cases, though the mix presents us with an acoustic drumset. It's clear that Watts is not playing live, but playfully poking a hole in the façade of the production. Even so, this video successfully inserts the band into the digital streaming space, while also appealing to an intimate connection with viewers. The musical intimacy here is grounded in the tone of the broadcast generally, which through fundraising, profiling of healthcare workers, and affect-laden musical performances tempered the severity of the pandemic and social isolation with a sense of the broader collective, that "we are all in this together," *Together Alone*.

Other videos from 2020 similarly draw attention to the façade of their liveness. For example, a *Today Show* performance of "We Got the Beat" features members of The Go-Gos each performing in their own homes ("The Go-Gos", 2020). Each band member has their own static, single-shot video squares, but the clip is extensively edited and fast-paced as these individual frames vary in size, number, and shape throughout the clip, zooming in and out of the televisual screen in various animated movements. While clearly not the original 1981 recording, the audio is professionally produced and mixed, which contrasts with the various domestic environments in which we see the musicians. Lead singer Belinda Carlisle delivers the vocals from her living room, drummer Gina Schock is behind her kit in a basement, guitarist and backing vocalist Jane Wiedlin plays in an outdoor area (with no visible guitar cable or wireless unit), bassist Kathy Valentine plays in front of a monochromatic digital background, and guitarist Charlotte Caffey plays in her living room. While the voices of Carlisle, Wiedlin, Valentine, and Caffey sing the chorus in unison, only Valentine has a visible vocal mic. This, along with the sonic uniformity of the individual contributions (we don't get a clashing amalgamation of ambient noise from these distinct environments, for example), suggests that the video utilizes a fully prerecorded audio track. That is, there is little effort put forth in this clip to mask the lack of liveness, which perhaps becomes secondary to the musical and visual aesthetics.

The economic and artistic upheaval wrought by the worldwide Covid-19 pandemic is reflected in the transition of many artists from live performance and touring spaces to digital performance environments. Aside from the relative entertainment value for audiences and perhaps a small revenue stream for artists, video performances during the Covid-19 pandemic offer a means for audiences and artists to engage and sustain their parasocial relationships. The connection here is primarily technological, and certainly many artists utilized social media and video platforms before Covid-19. However, what makes such content salient in the context of the pandemic is the added emphasis on connection, engagement, and intimacy. With the pandemic's enforced lack of not only live performance but social activity more generally, audiences arguably value the connection to artists through these engagements even more so than under normal circumstances. Moreover, the success of early Covid-era performance videos and livestreams is buoyed by the overt gestures to musical intimacy that they convey. The various tactics described in this section, including linguistic and bodily address, domestic framing, emphasis on familial relationships, as well as portrayals of intra-band intimacy, serve to humanize musical personae, reinforcing the perceived sense of intimate connection via parasocial interaction. Supported and strengthened by the technologies used in their creation, distribution, and consumption, the co-constructed parasocial relationships shared in musical performances during the Covid-19 pandemic can be especially endearing during a time when the sense of connection inherent in a traditional live performance is simply not possible.

Conclusion

In Chapter 1, we discussed commercial recording studios as sites of power in the construction of musical intimacy, where (often white, male) producers and engineers wield significant decision-making power in shaping the sound of popular music recordings, and how the resultant sonics seek to address, attract, and exploit intended audience demographics. Likewise in the context of performance, musical intimacy is often a deliberate construction, and one that underscores the power differentials between artists and audiences. Performance entails power in terms of both agency and domination, and is thus "a space where power is enacted, where audiences and performers negotiate and coordinate their behavior together in the context of sedimented practices" (Berger 2009: 124). Yet as Baym (2018: 110) argues, artists work "to control the sites where audiences engage in their fan practices and possibly the practices themselves." Here, Baym is referring to the myriad ways that an artist can seek to connect with fans online. However, her argument also speaks to artists' construction, reinforcement, and control of musical intimacy as engaged by musical personae and parasocial relationships. Although Auslander and Berger's emphasis on audience-performer negotiation are well taken, this is not typically a domain of equity and deliberation, as artists have far greater ability to control conditions of intimacy in performance. Even Horton and Wohl's (1956: 215) initial formulation of parasocial interactions emphasized their one-sided nature. Generally speaking, this is true of the performance context as well, be it in a shared physical space or a digital one. This lopsidedness is part of what makes parasocial relationships and thus musical intimacy possible, and strong musical personae are what make it effective.

The videos and livestreams that populated the internet during the Covid-19 pandemic are not creating musical personae from scratch. The performers mentioned in this chapter have established fan bases, and musical personae that have been crafted through decades of recorded output, concert tours, media publicity, and prior social media activity. Any lesser-known artist could follow these formulas and fail to establish a comparably strong parasocial bond. But as noted in our discussion of Bruce Springsteen, musical personae are unique compared to many other types of celebrity in that they do not take on wholly new "characters" with each project as a film actress does. The distinction between the musician's public and private identities is much more blurred, marking the musician's persona as uniquely "authentic," which can lay the foundation for the construction of a successful and intimate parasocial relationship (Kurtin et al. 2019: 31–3). Whether in an arena setting, a listening room, or via an Instagram livestream, the performance context consistently draws on elements of musical intimacy that, while constructed, may be perceived as authentic. And though authenticity is itself a murky and contested concept, it is ultimately what audiences are seeking in their engagement with musical intimacy. As a means of conclusion, the next chapter wrestles with questions of authenticity and musical intimacy to articulate why constructions of musical intimacy in popular music are so prevalent, and what value they serve for both artist and audience.

Conclusion

Throughout this book, we have examined musical intimacy and its many manifestations in popular music recording and performance, across multiple genres and contexts. Although our sample of objects for analysis is not by any means comprehensive, it does show the breadth and persistence of musical intimacy in popular music. However, we have yet to wrestle with the looming question of why. Why do music fans seek the physical intimacy of small venues? Why is there sustained interest in archival recordings and the uniquely intimate portraits that they can offer? Why are elements of intimacy a continued presence in commercially released recordings, from Fiona Apple to Sonny Rollins, from Prince to Taylor Swift?

A partial explanation for the persistence of musical intimacy may be the artistic, cultural, and personal value placed on authenticity, which is of central importance within media fandoms (Bennett 2017: 130; Hills 2002: 12). We argue that musical intimacy serves as a marker of such authenticity within popular music. Our purpose in this Conclusion is not to argue for a particular valuation or hierarchy of authentic forms of popular music. Such hierarchies of taste are somewhat arbitrary and tend to further entrench the marginalization of genres along lines of gender, race, and sexuality. Similarly, continued discourses of authenticity in popular music—as played out in music journalism and criticism—can reaffirm socio-cultural power dynamics in prescribing certain artists or work as inherently good because they are determined to be authentic (Weisethaunet and Lindberg 2010: 466). In contrast, we take a view of musical authenticity that centers audience agency and privileges listener perception.

Authenticity's reliance upon audience perception and subjectivity makes it a murky, multivalent concept. Despite this, the core of our various understandings of authenticity centers on the perceived "essential(ized), real, actual essence" of the work, object, or expression in question (Taylor 1997: 21). Likewise, because musical intimacy relies heavily on the perception of the listener, it is not an inherent quality of popular music recording or performance. Yet as noted throughout this book, certain characteristics, qualities, and styles do have recognized connotations of intimacy—the kinds of qualities that Moore labels "attributes of intimacy" (2002: 211).

Moore does not fully develop this idea, but it is a key point in considering musical intimacy and its connection to authenticity. Attributes of intimacy are crucial as those elements that build the rapport of musical intimacy, that engage listeners, and establish a sense of connection with the artist and their work. This book has discussed many such attributes, including inadvertent intimacies, the home recording aesthetic, musical personae, and the dimensions of musical intimacy discussed in Chapters 3 and 4. If successful, these gestures reinforce perceptions not only of intimacy, but of authenticity as well. Whatever the nature of a particular intimate encounter or relationship (romantic, sexual, physical, emotional, familial), the participants have access to parts of the other that few people typically do. In other words, we might feel that we know at least a piece of "the real person."

A similar principle is at play in some listeners' attraction to various manifestations of musical intimacy, and its ties to authenticity. If an artist's gestures of intimacy are perceived as sincere, transparent, and legitimate, listeners can feel that they've accessed a part of that person that is typically private, that through their music and performance, the artist is enacting their authentic identity rather than one that is purely performative. This is why Moore (2002: 214) argues that attributes of intimacy "are interpreted by an engaged audience as investing authenticity in those acts and gestures—the audience becomes engaged not with the acts and gestures themselves, but directly with the originator [performer] of those acts and gestures" (2002: 214). In other words, gestures of intimacy are a pathway that serves to reinforce perceptions of the authenticity of an artist, a performance, or a recording. Gestures of intimacy can of course run the spectrum from accidental to intentional, as noted in our discussion of inadvertent intimacies in Chapter 1. Regardless of intentionality, authenticity and musical intimacy are both constructions. This is not to say that intimacy and authenticity are simply matters of artifice, or that audiences who perceive authenticity and intimacy in popular music have fallen for an elaborate ruse. Authenticity and artifice are not diametric opposites, and even the artificial gesture can be perceived as valuable (Atton 2019; Moore 2002: 215).

In addition, perceptions of authenticity can be shaped by what information the listener brings to the musical encounter. Recalling our discussion in Chapter 2 for example, listeners may ascribe a certain amount of authenticity to home recordings simply due to their perceptions of artists being unencumbered by the constraints of a large format commercial studio, as well as the connotations of domestic spaces and intimacy. Listeners' knowledge of the technology used to create the recording can also play a role in shaping perceptions of authenticity. Seller (2019) notes that early critics of crooning considered the singing style inauthentic given its reliance on the electric microphone. Similar critiques abound throughout the history of popular music technology, including turntable scratching, drum machines, digital samplers, and, most recently, auto-tune (see Frith 1986, for example). Notably, perceptions of authenticity evolve over time, and as these examples suggest, technologies that might initially be criticized as inauthentic grow into acceptance. As new technological practices persist in popular music, they become normalized, while audiences acclimate to what was initially a novel sonic occurrence.

Perceptions of both authenticity and intimacy are not exclusively the purview of audiences, but we nonetheless argue that the audience is central. In the tradition of cultural studies' treatment of media audiences, we privilege reception as the site of meaning making, and by extension, of popular music's valuation. We do not suggest that such perceptions are uniform, given the polysemic nature of media texts. Even so, regardless of authorial intent, or whether an artist performs authentically and sincerely, what ultimately matters is whether audiences perceive the performance as authentic and sincere. Authentic and intimate musical experiences certainly get assistance from other parties in the musical process: songwriters, engineers, producers, performers, and promoters. But those experiences cannot be considered authentic or intimate until and unless audience members perceive them as such, imbuing them with that particular meaning and value.

In fact, audiences may well acknowledge that notions of authenticity (and by extension, intimacy) in popular music are constructions; yet, they may be invested enough in the success of a performance to suspend disbelief. Across a series of essays, Lawrence Grossberg discusses what he describes as the ideology of "authentic inauthenticity." Here, there is an open acknowledgment that authenticity is a construction (Grossberg 1993: 206). To that end, Weisethaunet and Lindberg (2010: 468) suggest that when we read musical performances as authentic, we may do so not because it is somehow pure and unmediated, but rather "it might also be that they are particularly well mediated." This paradox underscores that the perceived authenticity of a particular artist, performance, or recording can simply be the product of deliberate, strategic decisions in songwriting and recording aesthetics, alongside a carefully crafted persona that sells an authentic image. For Grossberg (1988: 58–9), the logic of authentic inauthenticity treats all texts and realities as equally deserving of serious attention, which ultimately makes difference between them both impossible and irrelevant. That is, no one particular construction of musical authenticity or intimacy has greater intrinsic value than any other; it is the listener's affective investment that affords value to these constructions (Grossberg 1986: 52).

In terms of authenticity in popular music, Moore (2002) suggests that we consider not *what* is authentic, but *whom*, and outlines three broad typologies of authentication in popular music; Moore's first- and second-person typologies are particularly relevant to our articulation of authenticity and musical intimacy. In first-person authenticity, the audience perceives the performer's emotional expression as authentic, while in second-person authenticity, the audience finds validation of their own emotions and experience through the artist's performance (Moore 2002: 214–20); or as Simon Frith (1996: 165) puts it, "songs are in this respect the narratives of our lives, of the ways in which we engage in—and realize—our fantasies."

As they relate to musical intimacy, these notions of first- and second-person authenticity recall our discussion of Bruce Springsteen in Chapter 6. As regards first-person authenticity, Springsteen's musical persona (itself framed around notions of authenticity and an "everyman" identity) works in concert with lyrics and performance that strive for sincerity, as well as the dimensions of recorded musical intimacy discussed in the book's first four chapters. (Think for, example, of 1982's *Nebraska* LP: a solo home four-track recording created for demo purposes, featuring a sparse mix of voice and acoustic guitar, with minimal overdubs.) Springsteen's persona also facilitates second-person authenticity, where audiences can perceive his lyrics centering on relationships, conflict, and working-class struggles as validating their own life experiences. This perceived relatability and sincerity can in turn foster a perceived mutuality or identification with Springsteen's musical persona (cf. Moore 2002). In short, for those fans who buy in, artists can leverage notions of authenticity in their work to also construct musical intimacy as a particular means of engagement between music, fans, performance, and persona.

Auslander (2021: 198) adds to this discussion that auteurship bolsters perceptions of authenticity in popular music. An ongoing body of work (as well as a sustained musical persona across that work) can serve to maintain the perceived relationship between artists and fans, while laying the groundwork for tangible perceptions of authenticity and intimacy within that relationship. This is evident in considering figures such as Springsteen or Beyoncé, who have built and maintained dedicated fan bases over a period of decades. In our current multiplatform world however, auteurship can develop in alternative ways, and across multiple outlets. Recalling our discussion of home recording in Chapter 2, Billie Eilish released her debut LP in 2019, but had by that point issued twelve singles and one EP both independently and through the Interscope label, along with placement in soundtracks and prominent streaming playlists. By the time of her full-length debut, Eilish had already amassed a dedicated fanbase across multiple releases, shaping her musical persona and auteurship in the process, both of which likely facilitated the perceived authenticity and intimacy of her debut album. All of this is to say that the current landscape of media and technology does not require artists to build up their auteur status over a period of decades alongside a mass audience; the ability to record, produce, distribute, and promote outside of traditional industry structures affords artists the opportunity to do so more swiftly, while engaging fans on multiple platforms.

Having accounted for the dynamics of auteurship and modes of authentication, this still begs the question of why we as listeners do buy in to a sense of authenticity and musical intimacy, even as we acknowledge their constructed nature. Assessing broader discourses of authenticity in popular culture, Michael Mario Albrecht (2008: 230) argues that "the idea of authenticity is appealing because it promises an experience that transcends the everyday in a society convinced that the banal is not enough ... [it is] something worth pursuing because it can lead to a more 'meaningful' experience." Refocusing Albrecht's argument to the context at hand, musical intimacy may not seem terribly extraordinary or transcendent. Musical intimacy is, at its core, about human relationality and connection—the very glue of everyday social life. Framed in this way, musical intimacy may, in fact, seem quite banal. However, we suggest two ways that as a marker of authenticity, musical intimacy transcends the banal in a manner aligned with Albrecht's claim.

The first of these is simply that despite being constructions, our relationships with musical personae do stand to transcend the intimacies and relations of our everyday lives and personal social circles. Listener relationships with celebrities and musical personae are by their very nature marked by distance—geographic, social, economic; part of the appeal of musical intimacy is that its various manifestations can be perceived as narrowing that gap. Whether it is recording techniques that place us into the intimate sonic space of the studio, emotionally compelling lyrics, or the *communitas* of a live performance, musical intimacy can transcend the everyday experience of music listening as a solitary activity and the characteristic disconnect between artist and listener. It is important to emphasize here that the listener's level of affective investment in the musical personae and their work drives the appeal and intensity of musical intimacy. It is difficult to imagine a case where a disinterested listener perceives (let alone values) musical intimacy in the work of an artist for whom they have no affective investment, or whom they actively dislike. As discussed in Chapter 5, musical intimacy is not exclusively the domain of actively engaged fandoms, but fans (as opposed to casual listeners) typically have far greater affective investment than does the casual listener, the disinterested listener, or the anti-fan (cf. Click 2019; Scott 2019). This allows for a deeper level of investment, as well as a unique relational engagement with the music, and by extension, the artist. Consequently, encounters with musical intimacy are likely to be more meaningful for devoted fans than other audience members.

Secondly, we return to Moore's (2002) framework of second-person authenticity. In this case, musical intimacy transcends the everyday experience of passive listening, as it requires active engagement, with outcomes that extend beyond mere pleasure, including increased affective intensity, and external validation of the listener's own experiences. In other words, markers of intimacy can serve as a means for listeners to acknowledge and process their own experiences, emotions, and thoughts as not in isolation, but through their relationality to the musical personae and the music itself. Our analysis of Fiona Apple's 2020 recording of "Fetch the Bolt Cutters" in Chapter 4 provides an especially clear example. As discussed in that chapter, Apple's recording features a number of sonic identifiers that mark the sonic space as domestic and organic, as opposed to the tightly controlled space of the professional recording studio. The aural intimacy of the sonic space, in conjunction with lyrics addressing confinement, and a progressively claustrophobic mix work in collaboration to build a unique and affectively intense recording that arguably transcends the aesthetic and affective "everydayness" typical of fully produced studio recordings. That so much of the press around Apple's album highlights its unique sonic palette points to this transcendence, which can have especially powerful resonance and validation for listeners who feel some sense of confinement in their everyday lives, be that emotional, physical, or psychological.

The cultural studies tradition and its progeny have long rejected the overly simplistic notion of media audiences as passive receptors in favor of understanding them as active agents within media culture. As discussed in this Conclusion and throughout the book, we take a similar view of popular music audiences. This can be frustrating from a social scientific point of view, as our understanding of musical intimacy leaves much in the hands of audience members and their individual perceptions; we cannot conclude this book with a strict, formulaic, generalizable prescription as to how musical intimacy operates across audiences. What we have presented, however, is an understanding of musical intimacy and how it can be constructed in the marketing, performance, and recording of popular music. In doing so, we stress the role of audience perception to center the listener as a productive agent of meaning making. Frith (1996: 203–4) reminds us that "listening itself is a performance," and that understanding how we engage in such performances is crucial to understanding popular music and culture. Musical intimacy is of course only a piece of that larger map of meaning and listening-as-performance, but it is one that we feel is important given the continued attention to intimacy in popular music culture and discourse, and its unique means of engagement between listeners, music, and artists.

Further, a better understanding of how musical intimacy is constructed and circulated also provides new insight into the affective dimensions of popular music. If, as Grossberg (1986: 52) suggests, "the power of music lies not in what it says, but what it does, in how it makes one move and feel," understanding the various manifestations of intimacy in popular music also clarifies a unique way that affect circulates between popular music listeners, texts, and performers—how particular sonics, musicological elements, or performance dynamics contribute to music's ability to give rise to feelings of engagement and closeness at a distance.

In contrast to other art forms, sound and music arguably "have a privileged relationship to affect" in light of their capacity for affect and mood modulation (Kassabian 2013: 179). This distinct facility, alongside music's ubiquity and the often-solitary act of music consumption frame music's relationship to listeners as characteristically intimate. That is, as a form, music is uniquely positioned to achieve intimacy. When that latent potential is brought to the fore, either by exploitative or by organic means, musical intimacy engenders a unique sense of connection and engagement. This is perhaps why across time periods, genres, and platforms, musical intimacy is a fixture of the popular music landscape that continues to resonate in our aural and affective fields.

Acknowledgments

There are two names on this book's cover, but it is of course the product of a constellation of individuals who have provided inspiration, resources, and support throughout the entire process.

Thanks firstly to all at Bloomsbury, especially Leah Babb-Rosenfeld and Rachel Moore whose guidance and support from proposal to publication were indispensable. Additionally, our reviewers' thorough feedback helped to refine the book's focus in its early stages.

This book has its roots in a series of conference presentations, where thoughtful and engaging discussions with other scholars provided valuable critiques and sparks of inspiration. We are especially grateful to Eric Abbey, Regina Bradley, Nick Artman, Kathryn Cox, De Angela Duff, Christine Feldman-Barrett, Anthony Kwame Harrison, Danielle Hidalgo, William McLean, Andrew Scott, and Suzanne Wint for their insight.

One of the under-acknowledged blessings of teaching is the inspiration, knowledge, and perspective that we get from our students. Many class discussions and informal conversations directly fed into this book. In that regard, we especially want to acknowledge Matthew Albright, Julia Amato, Amelia Atkins, Brianna Carter, Greg Davis, Sarah Everett, Allison Goodlin, Finn Kelly, Mike Kupris, Emily Loose, Andrew Lyn, Paul Miller, and Jeremy McCool.

Our personal networks of popular music scholars and like-minded music nerds were all too willing to discuss various stages of this project, read drafts, and offer examples and suggestions that helped us to overcome various hurdles and blindspots along the way. We are grateful for the colleagueship and friendship of Michael Mario Albrecht, Norma Coates, Michael Cunningham, Mike Duquette, Rebekah Farrugia, Mike Heyliger, Dave Lifton, Michael Parr, Ross Reilly, Kevin Shroth, Carrie Wittig, and Corey Wittig.

We must single out James Pobst, who read drafts of every chapter in *Musical Intimacy*, lending his keenly critical eye and robust, thoughtful feedback. We cannot understate his contributions to shaping the book at both the micro- and macro-levels.

Thanks also to past and present colleagues at Indiana University of Pennsylvania for their ongoing support, especially Mary Beth Leidman, Nurhaya Muchtar, Vicky Ortiz, Sue Rieg, and B. Gail Wilson.

We were fortunate to have had access to booksellers, collections, and interlibrary loan services that were crucial to locating and acquiring resources for our research, particularly during pandemic lockdowns. To that end, we are grateful to have had swift and knowledgeable assistance from folks at the Carnegie Library in Pittsburgh, the CC Mellor Library in Edgewood, PA, and the libraries at Indiana University of Pennsylvania.

Lastly, we thank our families and partners for their love and support throughout the course of writing this book, and always: Kate Lukaszewicz, Lisa Campbell, Katy Campbell, Nancy Stiegler, Bernie Stiegler, and Kristi Stiegler.

Notes

Introduction

1. On musical affordances, see Krueger (2011) and (2014).

Chapter 1

1. On John Bonham and the Speed King, see Welch and Nichols (2001).
2. Interestingly, this has been edited out, or at least mixed down in later reissues such as the 2012 compilation *50 Big Ones: Greatest Hits*.
3. This qualifying statement is a result of Mariah Carey's 1994 recording "All I Want for Christmas Is You," for which Carey received a production credit, and which spent its third consecutive week atop the Hot 100 in January 2020.

Chapter 2

1. ROMpler, a portmanteau of ROM (read only memory) and sampler, can be thought of as fixed sampler—one whose sounds are embedded in the architecture of the instrument and are usually only available for playback, with minimal options for alteration.
2. Gomez's reference to the remastered recording raises the point that remixed and remastered albums may alter musical intimacy through changing the sense of sonic space, or amplifying sounds that were buried in the previous mix. We discuss intimacy and reissues at greater depth in Chapter 5.
3. The liner notes tell us that other tracks on *Ghost~Pop* were recorded "in the living room," "in the bedroom," and "in the shower."

Chapter 3

1. Frith (1996: 191) uses the example of backup singers, whose very role is to support, but not distract from, the voice of the lead singer.

2 See also Chion's (1999: 165) similar notion of "vocal closeup."
3 A series of popular memes similarly play with sonic representation of space. Through EQ manipulation, these memes present listeners with specific spatial listening situations such as "Toto's 'Africa' (playing in an empty shopping centre)" and "The Cranberries' 'Linger' (playing from another room)." See Ward's (2021) compelling analysis.

Chapter 4

1 To clarify, this analysis utilizes Rudy Van Gelder's 2005 remaster of *Saxophone Colossus*.
2 Roach tuned his tom-toms for each individual track at this session. For "Blue 7," he tuned them to blend in with the song's tonal center, which further enables him to perform rhythmic and melodic ideas in conversation with the other players (Kenfield 1995: 166).
3 Prince's layered background vocals on the chorus are the only apparent overdubs on the released recording.
4 The gender of the addressee is clarified in the lyrics, as at (0:58–1:02) and (2:50–2:54).
5 An alternate version of the song (labeled "Take 2") was included in the 2019 Super Deluxe Edition of the *1999* album; the comparatively "dry" vocals in this alternate take suggest that the reverberation in the original release is an artificial application.
6 As Macel Ely II (2010: 99–109) writes, some form of the song was likely in circulation among the religious and folk cultures of the Appalachians much earlier; nevertheless, Brother Claude Ely was the first to copyright the song in 1954, and his origin story has been retold throughout the decades.
7 Since its release in 2010, Cash's recording of "Ain't No Grave" has appeared in *NCIS* (2010), *Wrestlemania XXVII* (2011), *Django Unchained* (2012), *Westworld* (2016), and *Pirates of the Caribbean: Dead Men Tell No Tales* (2017), among other media uses.
8 This lyrical passage was not present in Ely's recording, and may be an addition by Cash or Rubin.
9 This recalls the German expressionist technique of *sprechstimme*; this particular blurring of speaking and singing is perhaps most prominent in Schoenberg's *Pierrot Lunaire* (1912).
10 This occurs, for example, at 0:34, 1:20, 1:35, 1:46, 1:59, 2:18, 2:21, 2:24, 2:31, 2:34, 2:37, 2:41, 2:44, 2:50, 2:53–2:54, and 2:56–2:57.
11 Shot in her home studio, Apple performed "Fetch the Bolt Cutters" as part of the livestreamed New Yorker Festival in October 2020. In this performance of the song, she plays a floor tom, snare drum, and metal garbage can lid as the accompaniment to Amy Aileen Wood's brushed drumming.

12. Tim Carter (2001) explains tone-painting as "the musical representation of a work's broader emotional or other worlds … so as to express the dominant affection or image of the text."

Chapter 5

1. Reissues from Prince and Guns N' Roses demonstrate this kind of revisionism. In Prince's case, the "Vault" discs of the 2020 Super Deluxe edition of *1999* omitted two well-known recordings from the album sessions ("Extraloveable" and "Lust U Always") due to lyrical references to sexual violence. The Deluxe, Super Deluxe, and Locked n' Loaded editions of Guns N' Roses *Appetite for Destruction* included the 1988 *G n' R Lies* album, sans "One in a Million," a song long noted for its use of racial and sexual epithets.
2. The studio currently offers a remote mixing and mastering service, and has also licensed their trademark to numerous software platforms as plugins, in which "the legendary studio's signal chain is at your disposal—from the rooms in which magic happened, through the iconic vintage gear and techniques that ushered in the age of modern audio engineering" (Abbey Road Studios, Waves "Abbey Road Collection," Waves "Abbey Road Studio 3").

Chapter 6

1. To further underscore the emphasis on focused listening, promotional materials for many listening rooms also stress the quality of the house sound system and related gear. Many listening rooms go so far as to include a catalog of all equipment and associated technical specs. While this information may be of most interest to potential performers, it also demonstrates that the listening room takes sound quality seriously, in service of the music and of the audience's listening experience.
2. Though not a formal survey, in June 2020 we accessed publicly available information through the venue database at undiscoveredmusic.net, noted venues that self-identified as "listening rooms," and gathered information from their websites or direct inquiries as to venue capacity. Of approximately 613 venues listed, 84 explicitly identified themselves as listening rooms.
3. As of this writing, the clip is no longer available online.

References

20 Front Street. (n.d.), "20 Front Street." Available online: https://20frontstreet.com/ (accessed August 24, 2022).

Abbey Road Studios. (n.d.), "Online Mixing," Abbey Road Online. Available online: www.abbeyroad.com/online-mixing (accessed August 21, 2019).

Adams, Sam. (2020), "Fionna Apple's *Fetch the Bolt Cutters* is the Unofficial Album of the Pandemic," *Slate*, April 17, 2020. Available online: https://slate.com/culture/2020/04/fiona-apple-fetch-the-bolt-cutters-album-of-the-pandemic.html (accessed August 31, 2022).

Ake, David. (2010), *Jazz Matters: Sound, Place, and Time since Bebop*, Berkeley: University of California Press.

Albrecht, Michael Mario. (2008), "Fake Plastic Trees: Authenticity in Contemporary Popular Media Culture," PhD diss., University of Iowa, Iowa City.

Alleyne, Mike. (2022), "Unboxing the Box Set: Music Archives and Physical Formats in the Streaming Era," in *SAGE Business Cases*, London: SAGE Publications, Ltd. Available online: https://dx.doi.org/10.4135/9781529796063 (accessed August 31, 2022).

Als, Hilton. (2017), "'Springsteen on Broadway': Legends from a Life Story," *The New Yorker*, October 30. Available online: https://www.newyorker.com/magazine/2017/10/30/springsteen-on-broadway-legends-from-a-life-story (accessed August 31, 2022).

Altman, Rick. (1985), "The Technology of the Voice I: Part I," *Iris*, 3 (1): 3–20.

Altman, Rick. (1986), "The Technology of the Voice: Part II," *Iris*, 4 (1): 107–18.

Altman, Rick. (1992), "Afterword: A Baker's Dozen Terms for Sound Analysis," in Rick Altman (ed), *Sound Theory/Sound Practice*, 249–54, New York: Routledge.

Amburn, Ellis. (1995), *Buddy Holly: A Biography*, New York: St. Martin's Griffin Press.

Amir, Dorit. (1992), "Awakening and Expanding the Self: Meaningful Moments in the Music Therapy Process as Experienced and Described by Music Therapists and Music Therapy Clients," DA diss., New York University, New York.

"Ampex 200A 1947–1948," Museum of Magnetic Sound Recording. Available online: https://museumofmagneticsoundrecording.org/RecordersAmpex200A.html (accessed July 19, 2022).

Anderson, Benedict. (1983), *Imagined Communities: Reflections on the Origin and Spread of Nationalism*, London: Verso.

Ansdell, Gary. (2014), *How Music Helps in Music Therapy and Everyday Life*, Farrnham, England: Ashgate.

Apple, Fiona. (2020), "Fetch the Bolt Cutters" [song], on *Fetch the Bolt Cutters*, New York: Epic Records.

Aristotle. (1995), "On the Soul," in Jonathan Barnes (ed), *The Complete Works of Aristotle Volume One*, 641–92, Princeton: Princeton University Press.

Arlen, Michael J. (1980), *Thirty Seconds*, New York: Farrar, Straus and Giroux.

Arnheim, Rudolf. ([1986]/1936), *Radio*, London: Faber and Faber Ltd.

Arnold, Melvyn. (1975), "Music Therapy in a Transactional Analysis Setting," *Journal of Music Therapy*, 12 (3): 104–20.

Askerøi, Eirik. (2013), "Reading Pop Production: Sonic Markers and Musical Identity," PhD diss., University of Agder, Kristiansand.

Aswad, Jem. (2020), "Concert Industry Lost $30 Billion in 2020," *Variety*, December 11. Available online: https://variety.com/2020/music/news/concert-industry-lost-30-billion-2020-1234851679/

Attali, Jacques. ([1985]/2003), *Noise: The Political Economy of Music*, Minneapolis: University of Minneapolis Press.

Atton, Chris. (2019), "Challenging Authenticity: Fakes and Forgeries in Rock Music," *Popular Music*, 38 (2): 204–18.

Auslander, Philip. (2006), "Musical Personae," *The Drama Review*, 50 (1): 100–19.

Auslander, Philip. (2008), *Liveness: Performance in a Mediatized Culture*, 2nd edn, London: Routledge.

Auslander, Philip. (2012), "Digital Liveness: A Historico-Philosophical Perspective," *PAJ: A Journal of Performance and Art*, 34 (3): 3–11.

Auslander, Philip. (2021), *In Concert: Performing Musical Persona*, Ann Arbor: University of Michigan Press.

Austin, Diane. (2002), "The Voice of Trauma: A Wounded Healer's Perspective," in Julie Sutton (ed), *Music, Music Therapy, and Trauma: International Perspectives*, 231–58, London: Jessica Kinglsey Publishers.

Auter, Philip. (1992), "TV that Talks Back: An Experimental Validation of a Parasocial Interaction Scale," *Journal of Broadcasting and Electronic Media*, 36 (2): 173–81.

Auter, Philip J. and D. M. Davis. (1991), "When Characters Speak Directly to Viewers: Breaking the Fourth Wall in Television," *Journalism Quarterly*, 68 (102): 165–71.

Auter, Philip J. and Philip Palmgreen. (2000), "Development and Validation of a Parasocial Interaction Measure: The Audience-Persona Interaction Scale," *Communication Research Reports*, 17 (1): 79–890.

Balkwill, Laura-Lee and William Forde Thompson. (1999), "A Cross-Cultural Investigation of the Perception of Emotion in Music: Psychophysical and Cultural Cues," *Music Perception*, 17 (1): 43–64.

Ballentine, Paul W. and Brett A. S. Martin. (2005), "Forming Parasocial Relationships in Online Communities," *Advances in Consumer Research*, 32 (1): 197–201.

Barret, Frederick S., Kevin J. Grimm, Richard W. Robins, Tim Wildschut, Constantine Sedikides, and Petr Janata. (2010), "Music-Evoked Nostalgia: Affect, Memory, and Personality," *Emotion*, 10 (3): 309–403.

Barthes, Roland. (1977), "The Grain of the Voice," in Stephen Heath (trans), *Image Music Text*, 179–89, New York: Hill and Wang.

Baym, Nancy. (2018), *Playing to the Crowd: Musicians, Audiences, and the Intimate Work of Connection*, New York: NYU Press.

Baym, Nancy, Daniel Cavicchi, and Norma Coates. (2018), "Music Fandom in the Digital Age: A Conversation," in Melissa A. Click and Suzanne Scott (eds), *The Routledge Companion to Media Fandom*, 141–52, New York: Routledge.

"Beach Boys SMiLE Unboxing," [video] The Beach Boys, August 29, 2011. Available online: https://youtu.be/fvB0glRsolw (accessed August 23, 2022).

Beach, Lee. (2018), "Springsteen as Post-Christian Pastor," *BOSS: The Biannual Online-Journal of Springsteen Studies*, 3 (1): 60–89.

"Beatles Anthology Ad 1995," [video] Sola174, February 6, 2011. Available online: youtu.be/eXWDcBYOIFs (accessed September 7, 2020).

Beebe, Steven. A., Susan J. Beebe, and Mark V. Redmond. (2010), *Interpersonal Communication: Relating to Others*, 6th edn, Boston: Pearson.

Beekhuyzen, Jenine, Lisa von Hellens, and Sue Nielsen. (2011), "Underground Online Music Communities: Exploring Rules for Membership," *Online Information Review*, 35 (5): 699–715.

Belfi, Amy M., Brett Karlan, and Daniel Tranel. (2015), "Music Evokes Vivid Autobiographical Memories," *Memory*, 24 (7): 979–89.

Bell, Adam Patrick. (2015), "DAW Democracy? The Dearth of Diversity in 'Playing the Studio,'" *Journal of Music, Technology, and Education*, 8 (2): 129–46.

"Ben Ellman on Producing Walter 'Wolfman' Washington's New Album" [podcast episode], *It's a Good Life, Babe*, April 18, 2018. Available online: http://www.itsagoodlifebabe.com/glb/2018/4/19/ep102-ben-ellman-on-producing-walter-wolfman-washingtons-new-album-the-house-mans-green-room-s (accessed July 13, 2021).

Bennett, Lucy. (2014), "'If We Stick Together, We Can Do Anything': Lady Gaga Fandom, Philanthropy, and Activism through Social Media," *Celebrity Studies*, 5 (1–2): 138–52.

Bennett, Lucy. (2017), "Resisting Technology in Music Fandom: Nostalgia, Authenticity, and Kate Bush's 'Before the Dawn,'" in Jonathan Gray, Cornel Sandvoss, and C. Lee Harrington (eds), *Fandom: Identities and Communities in a Mediated World*, 2nd edn, 127–42, New York: NYU Press.

Bennett, Samantha. (2016), "Behind the Magical Mystery Door: History, Mythology, and the Aura of Abbey Road Studios," *Popular Music*, 35 (3): 396–417.

Berger, Harris M. (2009), *Stance: Ideas about Emotion, Style, and Meaning for the Study of Expressive Culture*, Middletown: Wesleyan University Press.

Berlant, Lauren. (2000), "Intimacy: A Special Issue," in Lauren Berlant (ed), *Intimacy*, 1–8, Chicago: University of Chicago Press.

Berliner, Paul F. (1994), *Thinking in Jazz: The Infinite Art of Improvisation*, Chicago: University of Chicago Press.

Bernhagen, Linday M. (2013), "Sounding Subjectivity: Music, Gender, and Intimacy," PhD diss., Ohio State University, Columbus.

Bernasi, Leo and Adam Phillips. (2008), *Intimacies*, Chicago: University of Chicago Press.

Berryman, Rachel and Misha Kavka. (2017), "'I Guess a Lot of People See Me as a Big Sister or a Friend': The Role of Intimacy in the Celebrification of Beauty Vloggers," *Journal of Gender Studies*, 26 (3): 307–20.

Bharucha, Jamshed J., Meagan Curtis, and Kaivon Paroo. (2006), "Varieties of Musical Experience," *Cognition*, 100 (1): 131–72.

Biddle, Ian. (2013), "Quiet Sounds and Intimate Listening: The Politics of Tiny Seductions," in Marie Thompson and Ian Biddle (eds), *Sound Music Affect: Theorizing Sonic Experience*, 205–22, London: Bloomsbury.

"Billie Eilish Is a Different Kind of Pop Star," [podcast episode] *Switched on Pop*, April 9, 2019. Available online: https://switchedonpop.com/episodes/billie-eilish-is-a-different-kind-of-pop-star (accessed August 31, 2022).

"Billie Joe Armstrong with His Sons – I Think We're Alone Now," [video] Kevin Richards, April 30, 2020. Available online: https://youtu.be/2QnHjkBD_YI (accessed August 24, 2022).

Bird, Elizabeth. (1994), "'Is that Me, Baby?' Image, Authenticity, and the Career of Bruce Springsteen," *American Studies*, 35 (2): 39–57.

Bon Iver. (2007), *For Emma, Forever Ago* [album], London: 4AD.

Borin, Kim and Abby L. Dvorak. (2018), "Music Therapy and Intimacy Behaviors of Hospice Family Caregivers in South Korea: A Randomized Crossover Clinical Trial," *Nordic Journal of Music Therapy*, 27 (3): 218–34.

Bottomley, Andrew J. (2016), "Play It Again: Rock Music Reissues and the Production of the Past for the Present," *Popular Music and Society*, 39 (2): 151–74.

Boym, Sventlana. (2001), *The Future of Nostalgia*, New York: Basic Books.

Brennan, Teresa. (2004), *The Transmission of Affect*, Ithaca: Cornell University Press.

Brøvig-Hanssen, Ragnhild. (2013), "Music in Bits and Bits of Music: Signatures of Digital Mediation in Popular Music Recordings," PhD diss., University of Oslo, Oslo.

Brøvig-Hanssen, Ragnhild and Anne Danielsen. (2013), "The Naturalized and the Surreal: Changes in the Perception of Popular Music Sound," *Organized Sound*, 18 (1): 71–80.

Bruford, Bill. (2019). Personal communication with author, 25 February.

Bugle Boy. (n.d.), "The Listening Room." Available online: https://thebugleboy.org/the-listening-room/ (accessed August 24, 2022).

Burgess, Jean and Joshua Green. (2018), *YouTube: Online Video and Participatory Culture*, Cambridge: Polity.

Campion, James. (2015), *Shout It Out Loud: The Story of Kiss's Destroyer and the Making of an American Icon*, Milwaukee: Backbeat Books.

Carlin, Peter Ames. (2012), *Bruce*, New York: Touchstone.

Carpenter, Edmund and Marshall McLuhan. (1960), "Acoustic Space," in Edmund Carpenter and Marshall McLuhan (eds), *Explorations in Communication*, 65–70, Boston: Beacon Press.

Carter, Tim. (2001), "Word-painting," *Oxford Music Online*. Available online: https://doi.org/10.1093/gmo/9781561592630.article.30568 (accessed August 31, 2022).

de Carvalho, Alice Tomaz. (2012), "The Discourse of Home Recording: Authority of Pros and the Sovereignty of the Big Studios," *Journal of the Art of Record Production*, 7.

Cash, Johnny. (2010), "Ain't No Grave" [song], on *American VI: Ain't No Grave*, Santa Monica: American Recordings.

Cash, Johnny and Patrick Carr. (1997), *Cash: The Autobiography*, New York: Harper San Francisco.

Castellano, Mary A., J. J. Bharucha, and Carol L. Krumhansl. (1984), "Tonal Hierarchies in the Music of North India," *Journal of Experimental Psychology: General*, 113 (3): 394–412.

Caughey, John L. (1986), "Social Relations with Media Figures," in Gary Gumpert and Robert Cathcart (eds), *Inter Media: Interpersonal Communication in a Media World*, 3rd edn, 219–52, New York: Oxford University Press.

Cavarero, Adriana. (2005), *For More Than One Voice: Toward a Philosophy of Vocal Expression*, trans. Paul A. Kottman, Stanford: Stanford University Press.

Cavicchi, Daniel. (1998), *Tramps Like Us: Music and Meaning among Springsteen Fans*, Oxford: Oxford University Press.

Chen, Chih-Ping. (2014), "Forming Digital Self and Parasocial Relationships on YouTube," *Journal of Consumer Culture*, 16 (1): 232–54.

Chick, Stevie. (2005), "The White Stripes: Heart of Darkness," *Mojo*, August. Available online: https://steviechick.wordpress.com/2018/09/13/the-white-stripes-in-brazil-2005/ (accessed August 31, 2022).

Chion, Michel. (1999), *The Voice in Cinema*, trans. Claudia Gorbman, New York: Columbia University Press.

Click, Melissa, (ed) (2019), *Anti-Fandom: Dislike and Hate in the Digital Age*, New York: NYU Press.

Clinebell, Howard J. and Charlotte H. Clinebell. (1970), *The Intimate Marriage*, New York: Harper and Row.

Colton, Lisa. (2014), "Who's Calling? Telephone Songs, Female Vocal Empowerment and Signification," in Martin Iddon and Melanie Marshall (eds), *Lady Gaga and Popular Music: Performing Gender, Fashion, and Culture*, 67–81, New York: Routledge.

Connor, Steven. (1997), *Postmodernist Culture: An Introduction to Theories of the Contemporary*, 2nd edn, Oxford: Blackwell Publishers.

Cook-Wilson, Winston. (2018), "Prince's Playful 'Piano and a Microphone 1983' is an Intimate Peek into a Master's Process," *Spin*, September 24. Available online: https://www.spin.com/2018/09/prince-piano-and-a-microphone-1983-review/ (accessed August 23, 2022).

Corcoran, Nina. (2020), "With Fetch the Bolt Cutters, Fiona Apple Hits a Zenith of Liberation and Experimentation," *The A.V. Club*, April 17. Available online: https://music.avclub.com/with-fetch-the-bolt-cutters-fiona-apple-hits-a-zenith-1842908893 (accessed August 31, 2022).

Couldry, Nick. (2004), "Liveness, 'Reality', and the Mediated Habitus from Television to the Mobile Phone," *The Communication Review*, 7 (4): 353–61.

Cowie, Jefferson and Lauren Bohem. (2016), "Dead Man's Town: 'Born in the USA', Social History, and Working-Class Identity," in Kenneth Womack, Jerry Zoltan, and Mark Bernhard (eds), *Bruce Springsteen, Cultural Studies, and the Runaway American Dream*, 25–44, London: Routledge.

Crane, Larry. (2022), "Jacknife Lee: Looking for Noise," *Tape Op* 149: 33–40.

Crockett, Zachary. (2016), "Tiny Desk: How NPR's Intimate Concert Series Earned a Cult Following," *Vox*, November 21. Available online: https://www.vox.com/culture/2016/11/21/13550754/npr-tiny-desk-concert (accessed August 31, 2022).

Crooks, John. (2012), "Recreating an Unreal Reality: Performance Practice, Recording, and the Jazz Rhythm Section," *Journal on the Art of Record Production*, 6.

"Sheryl Crow – All I Wanna Do (Quarantine Edition)," [video] Sheryl Crow, April 24, 2020. Available online: https://youtu.be/lhFGuWWlmGY (accessed August 24, 2022).

Crowther, Gail and Peter K. Steinberg. (2017), *These Ghostly Archives: The Unearthing of Sylvia Plath*, Stroud: Fonthill Media.

Cummings, Kamilah. (2020), "Prince: Introduction of a New Breed Leader," in Mike Alleyne and Kirsty Fairclough (eds), *Prince and Popular Music: Critical Perspectives on an Interdisciplinary Life*, 161–74, New York: Bloomsbury Academic.

Cummins, R. Glenn and Boni Cui. (2014), "Reconceptualizing Address in Television Programming: The Effect of Address and Affective Empathy on Viewer Experience on Parasocial Interaction," *Journal of Communication*, 4 (64): 723–42.

Cusick, Suzanne G. (2006), "On a Lesbian Relationship with Music: A Serious Effort Not to Think Straight," in Philip Brett, Elizabeth Wood, and Gary C. Thomas (eds), *Queering the Pitch: The New Gay and Lesbian Musicology*, 2nd edn, 67–85, New York: Routledge.

Daly, Rhian. (2019), "Billie Eilish's Brother/Collaborator Finneas Reveals the Secrets within the Record-Breaking Debut Album," *NME*, April 11. Available online: https://www.nme.com/blogs/nme-radar/billie-eilish-album-brother-and-producer-finneas-interview-2475296 (accessed August 31, 2022).

Damasio, Antonio R. (1994), *Descartes' Error: Emotion, Reason, and the Human Brain*, New York: Avon Books.

Dansby, Andrew. (2001), "Johnny Cash Leaves Hospital," *Rolling Stone*, October 23. Available online https://www.rollingstone.com/music/music-news/johnny-cash-leaves-hospital-242817/ (accessed August 31, 2022).

Dewey, John. (1934), *Art as Experience*, New York: Perigee Books.

Dibben, Nicola. (2003), "Musical Materials, Perception, and Listening," in Martin Clayton, Trevor Herbert, and Richard Middleton (eds), *The Cultural Study of Music: A Critical Introduction*, 193–203, New York: Routledge.

van Dijk, Jose. (2006), "Record and Hold: Popular Music between Personal and Collective Memory," *Critical Studies in Media Communication*, 23 (5): 357–74.

Dockwray, Ruth and Allan F. Moore. (2010), "Configuring the Sound-Box 1965–1972," *Popular Music*, 29 (2): 181–97.

Dolar, Mladen. (2006), *A Voice and Nothing More*, Cambridge: MIT Press.

Douglas, Susan. (2004), *Listening in: Radio and the American Imagination*, Minneapolis: University of Minnesota Press.

Doyle, Peter. (2005), *Echo and Reverb: Fabricating Space in Popular Music Recording, 1900–1960*, Middletown: Wesleyan University Press.

Duffett, Mark. (2013), *Understanding Fandom: An Introduction to the Study of Media Fan Culture*, New York: Bloomsbury.

Duffett, Mark. (2014a), "Introduction," in Mark Duffett (ed), *Popular Music Fandom: Identities, Roles, and Practices*, 1–15, New York: Routledge.

Duffett, Mark. (2014b), "Fan Words," in Mark Duffett (ed), *Popular Music Fandom: Identities, Roles, and Practices*, 146–64, New York: Routledge.

Duffett, Mark. (2017), "I Scream Therefore I Fan? Music Audiences and Affective Citizenship," in Jonathan Gray, Cornel Sandvoss, and C. Lee Harrington (eds), *Fandom: Identities and Communities in a Mediated World*, 2nd edn, 143–56, New York: NYU Press.

Duncan, Robert. (1978), "Lawdamercy, Springsteen Saves!" *Creem*, 5 (10): 39–43, 64–6.

Edwards, Jane. (2011), "The Use of Music Therapy to Promote Attachment between Parents and Infants," *The Arts in Psychotherapy*, 38 (3): 190–5.

Ely, Macel. (2010), *Ain't No Grave: The Life and Legacy of Brother Claude Ely*, Atlanta: Dust to Digital.

Eno, Brian. ([1979]/2017), "The Studio as Compositional Tool," in Christoph Cox and Daniel Warner (eds), *Audio Culture: Readings in Modern Music*, 2nd edn, 185–96, New York: Bloomsbury.

Esposito, Anthony and Ronald K. Raymond. (2018), "Springsteen and I: A Documentary Analysis of Springsteen's Fan Base," *BOSS: The Biannual Online-Journal of Springsteen Studies*, 3 (1): 90–106.

Fast, Susan. (2001), *Houses of the Holy: Led Zeppelin and the Power of Rock Music*, Oxford: Oxford University Press.

Feldman, Christine Jacqueline. (2009), *We Are the Mods: A Transnational History of a Youth Subculture*, New York: Peter Lang.

Fensterstock, Alison. (2020), "The Unexpected Coziness of the Las Vegas Residency," *Vice*, February 3. Available online: https://www.vice.com/en_us/article/qjdv5p/las-vegas-residency-history (accessed August 30, 2022).

Figlerowicz, Marta. (2012), "Affect Theory Dossier: An Introduction," *Qui Parle*, 20 (2): 3–18.

"Down on the Corner – Cosmo's Factory/Fogerty's Factory," [video] John Fogerty, April 6, 2020. Available online: https://youtu.be/fduevUJtsv4 (accessed August 24, 2022).

Frith, Simon. (1986), "Art versus Technology: The Strange Case of Popular Music," *Media, Culture, and Society*, 8 (3): 263–790.

Frith, Simon. (1988), *Music for Pleasure: Essays on the Sociology of Pop*, London: Routledge.

Frith, Simon. (1996), *Performing Rites: On the Value of Popular Music*, Cambridge: Harvard University Press.

Frith, Simon. (2013), "The Real Thing—Bruce Springsteen," in Theo Cateforis (ed), *The Rock History Reader*, 2nd edn, 253–60, New York: Routledge.

Froude, James Anthony. (1876), *Caesar: A Sketch*, New York: Charles Scribner's Sons.

Gabrielsson, Alf and Erik Lindström. (2010), "The Role of Structure in the Musical Expression of Emotions," in Patrik Juslin and John Sloboda (eds), *Handbook of Music and Emotion: Theory, Research, Applications*, 367–400, Oxford: Oxford University Press.

Gabrielsson, Alf and Erik Lindström. (2011), "The Influence of Musical Structure on Emotional Expression," in Patrik Juslin and John Sloboda (eds), *Handbook of Music and Emotion: Theory, Research, Applications*, 223–48, Oxford: Oxford University Press.

Gadlin, Howard. (1977), "Private Lives and Public Order: A Critical View of the History of Intimate Relations in the United States," in George Levenger and Harold L. Raush (eds), *Close Relationships: Perspectives on the Meaning of Intimacy*, 33–72, Amherst: University of Massachusetts Press.

Garbarini, Vic. (2000), "Police Reunion! The Members of The Police Grant Their First Joint Interview since Parting Ways More Than 15 Years Ago," *Revolver*, Available online: https://ho.sting.com/news/title/Interview:%20REVOLVER%20(2000) (accessed August 31, 2022).

Garcia, Luis-Manuel. (2011), "'Can You Feel It Too?': Intimacy and Affect at Electronic Dance Music Events in Paris, Chicago, and Berlin," PhD diss., University of Chicago, Chicago.

Garelick, Jon. (2019), "Bruce Springsteen Mastered Audience Engagement before It Was a Term, and His New Album Keeps It Up," *NBC News*, June 17. Available online:https://www.nbcnews.com/think/opinion/bruce-springsteen-mastered-audience-engagement-it-was-term-his-new-ncna1017286 (accessed August 31, 2022).

Geraghty, Lincoln. (2018), "Class, Capital, and Collecting in Media Fandom," in Melissa A. Click and Suzanne Scott (eds), *The Routledge Companion to Media Fandom*, 212–20, New York: Routledge.

Gibson, J. J. (1979), *The Ecological Approach to Visual Perception*, Hillsdale: Lawrence Erlbaum Associates.

Givan, Benjamin. (2014), "Gunther Schuller and the Challenge of Sonny Rollins: Stylistic Context, Intentionality, and Jazz Analysis," *Journal of the American Musicological Society*, 67 (1): 167–237.

Gleason, Ralph J. (1957), "Sonny Rollins: Saxophone Colossus," *Downbeat*, June 27. Available online: https://downbeat.com/microsites/prestige/sonny-review-colossus.html (accessed August 31, 2022).

Goffman, Erving. (1959), *The Presentation of Self in Everyday Life*, New York: Doubleday.

"The Go-Gos – We Got the Beat (Live from the Today Show/2020," [video] Official Gogos, 18 September 2020). Available online: https://youtu.be/GNcfx2dx9_8 (accessed August 24, 2022).

Gomez, Jade. (2020), "Elliott Smith's Classic Self-Titled LP Is Revitalized on New Anniversary Edition," *Paste Magazine*, September 3. Available online: https://www.pastemagazine.com/music/elliott-smith/self-titled-debut-album-anniversary-review/ (accessed August 31, 2022).

Goold, Lachlan and Phil Graham. (2019), "The Uncertain Future of the Large-Format Recording Studio," in J-O Gullö (ed), *Proceedings of the 12th Art of Record Production Conference*, 19–136, Stockholm: Royal College of Music and Art of Record Production.

Gracyk, Theodore. (1996), *Rhythm and Noise: An Aesthetics of Rock*, Durham: Duke University Press.

Gracyk, Theodore. (1997), "Listening to Music: Performances and Recordings," *Journal of Aesthetics and Art Criticism*, 55 (2): 139–50.

Grainge, Paul. (2002), *Monochrome Memories: Nostalgia and Style in Retro America*, Westport: Praeger.

Graver, David. (1997), "The Actor's Bodies," *Text and Performance Quarterly*, 17 (3): 221–35.

Graver, William W. (1991), "Technology Affordances," *Proceedings of the Conference on Human Factors in Computing Systems*. Available online: DOI: 10.1145/108844.108856 (accessed August 31, 2022).

Greene, Andy. (2017), "Review: Bruce Springsteen's Broadway Show Is an Intimate Triumph," *Rolling Stone*, October 13. Available online: https://www.rollingstone.com/music/music-live-reviews/review-bruce-springsteens-broadway-show-is-an-intimate-triumph-196969/ (accessed August 31, 2022).

Grossberg, Lawrence. (1984), "Another Boring Day in Paradise: Rock and Roll and the Empowerment of Everyday Life," *Popular Music*, 4: 225–58.

Grossberg, Lawrence. (1986), "Is there Rock after Punk?" *Critical Studies in Media Communication*, 3 (1): 50–74.

Grossberg, Lawrence. (1988), "Pedagogy in the Age of Reagan: Politics, Postmodernity, and the Popular," *Curriculum and Teaching*, 3: 47–62.

Grossberg, Lawrence. (1989), "Putting the Pop Back into Postmodernism," *Social Text*, 21: 167–90.

Grossberg, Lawrence. (1993), "The Media Economy of Rock Culture: Cinema, Post-Modernity and Authenticity," in Simon Frith, Andrew Goodwin, and Lawrence Grossberg (eds), *Sound and Vision: The Music Video Reader*, 185–209, London: Routledge.

Grow, Kory. (2018), "Review: Prince's 'Piano and a Microphone 1983' Is a Revealing Snapshot of the Pop Genius in His Prime," *Rolling Stone*, September 21. Available online: https://www.rollingstone.com/music/music-album-reviews/review-princes-piano-a-microphone-1983-is-a-revealing-snapshot-of-the-pop-genius-in-his-prime-727216/ (accessed August 31, 2022).

Hagen, William Ross. (2010), "Fandom: Participatory Music Behavior in the Age of Postmodern Media," PhD diss., University of Colorado, Boulder.

Hagood, Mack. (2019), *Hush: Media and Sonic Self-Control*, Durham: Duke University Press.

Hall, Edward T. (1963), "A System for the Notation of Proxemic Behavior," *American Anthropologist*, 65 (5): 1003–26.

Hall, Edward T. (1969), *The Hidden Dimension: An Anthropologist Examines Man's Use of Space in Public and Private*, Garden City: Anchor Books.

Handler, Rachel. (2020), "Allow Fiona Apple to Reintroduce Herself," *Vulture*, April 17. Available online: https://www.vulture.com/2020/04/fiona-apple-fetch-the-bolt-cutters.html (accessed August 31, 2022).

Hartmann, Tilo and Charlotte Goldhoorn. (2011), "'Horton and Wohl Revisited: Exploring Viewers' Experience of Parasocial Interaction," *Journal of Communication*, 61 (6): 1104–21.

Hartmann, Tilo and Christoph Klimmt. (2005), "Ursachen und Effekte Parasozialer Interaktionen im Rezeptionsprozess: Eine Fragebogenstudie auf der Basis des PSI-Zwei-Ebenen-Modells [Causes and consequences of parasocial interaction]," *Zeitschrift für Medienpsychologie*, 17 (3): 88–98.

Harvey, S. (2022), "Finneas on Producing Billie Eilish's Hit Album in His Bedroom," July 5. Available online: https://www.mixonline.com/recording/finneas-on-producing-billie-eilishs-number-one-album-in-his-bedroom (accessed August 31, 2022).

Hatfield, Elaine. (1982), "Passionate Love, Compassionate Love, and Intimacy," in Martin Fisher and George Stricker (eds), *Intimacy*, 267–92, New York: Plenum Press.

Hayes, Joy and Dana Gravesen. (2013), "Body Contact: Interconnection and Embodiment in Howard Stern's 9/11 Radio Broadcast," in Joy Elizabeth Hayes, Kathleen Battles, and Wendy Hilton-Morrow (eds), *War of the Worlds to Social Media: Mediated Communication in Times of Crisis*, 142–63, New York: Peter Lang.

Hemphill, Michael R. and Larry David Smith. (1990), "The Working American's Elegy: The Rhetoric of Bruce Springsteen," in Robert L. Savage and Dan Nimmo (eds), *Politics in Familiar Contexts*, 199–214, Norwood: Praeger Publishers.

Hendler, Glenn. (2020), *Diamond Dogs*, New York: Bloomsbury Academic.

Herrera, David. (2017), "Parasocial Engagement for Musicians and Artists: A Systemic Review of Theoretical Foundations with Applications," *Journal of the Music and Entertainment Industry Educators Association*, 17 (1): 13–30.

Hills, Matt. (2002), *Fan Cultures*, London: Routledge.

Hilmes, Michelle. (1997), *Radio Voices: American Broadcasting 1922–1952*, Minneapolis: University of Minneapolis Press.

Horton, Donald and R. Richard Wohl. (1956), "Mass Communication and Para-Social Interaction: Observations on Intimacy at a Distance," *Psychiatry*, 19 (3): 215–29.

Hyden, Steven. (2018), *Twilight of the Gods: A Journey to the End of Classic Rock*, New York: HarperCollins.

"Intimate." (2005), *Urban Dictionary*. Available online: https://www.urbandictionary.com/define.php?term=intimate (accessed August 31, 2022).

Jameson, Frederic. (1991), *Postmodernism or, the Cultural Logic of Late Capitalism*, Durham: Duke University Press.

Janata, Petr, Stefan T. Tomic, and Sonja K. Rakowksi. (2007), "Characterisation of Music-Evoked Autobiographical Memories," *Memory*, 15 (8): 845–60.

Jarman, Freya. (2013), "Relax, Feel Good, Chill Out: The Affective Distribution of Classical Music," in Marie Thompson and Ian Biddle (eds), *Sound Music Affect: Theorizing Sonic Experience*, 183–204, London: Bloomsbury.

Jarvenpaa, Sirkka L. and Karl R. Lang. (2011), "Boundary Management in Online Communities: Case Studies of the Nine Inch Nails and ccMixter Music Remix Sites," *Long Range Planning*, 44 (5–6): 440–57.

Jenkins, Henry. (2003), *The WOW Climax: Tracing the Emotional Impact of Popular Culture*. New York: NYU Press.

Jerslev, Anne. (2016), "In the Time of Microcelebrity: Celebrification and the YouTuber Zoella," *International Journal of Communication*, 10: 5233–51.

Johansson, Mats. (2012), "Michael Jackson and the Expressive Power of Voice-Produced Sound," *Popular Music and Society*, 35 (2): 261–79.

"John Legend - #TogetherAtHome Concert Series," [video] John Legend, March 18, 2020. Available online: https://youtu.be/I2NTcBmQkjw (accessed August 24, 2022).

Johnston, Jessica. (2017), "Subscribing to Sex Edutainment: Sex Education, Online Video, and the YouTube Star," *Television and New Media*, 18 (1): 76–92.

JPEGMAFIA. [@jpegmafia]. (2020). "I Won't Lie … Some of My Old Shit Is Hard to Hear Now … Especially the Ghost Pop Tape. I Was," [Tweet]. Twitter, March 5. Available online: https://twitter.com/jpegmafia/status/1418490125101662208 (accessed August 31, 2022).

Karst, Kenneth. (1980), "The Freedom of Intimate Association," *Yale Law Journal*, 89 (4): 624–92.

Kassabian, Anahid. (2013), "Music for Sleeping," in Marie Thompson and Ian Biddle (eds), *Sound Music Affect: Theorizing Sonic Experience*, 165–81, London: Bloomsbury.

Kassing, Jeffrey W. and Jimmy Sanderson. (2009), "'You're the Kind of Guy That We All Want for a Drinking Buddy': Expressions of Parasocial Interaction on Floydlandis.com," *Journal of Communication*, 73 (2): 182–203.

Kawakami, Ai, Kiyoshi Furukawa, Kentaro Katahira, Keiko Kamiyama, and K. Kazuo Okanoya (2012), "Relations between Musical Structures and Perceived and Felt Emotions," *Music Perception: An Interdisciplinary Journal*, 30 (4): 407–17.

Kenfield, Barry. (1995), *What to Listen for in Jazz*. New Haven: Yale University Press.

Kerns, David. (2012), "Springsteen in Concert: The Magic Ingredient," *Napa Valley Register*, Available online: https://napavalleyregister.com/entertainment/article_37d87378-9a40-11e1-b400-0019bb2963f4.html (accessed August 31).

Kessler, Edward J., Christa Hansen, and Roger N. Shepard. (1984), "Tonal Schemata in the Perception of Music in Bali and in the West," *Music Perception*, 2 (2): 131–65.

Kingsbury, Henry. (1988), *Music, Talent and Performance: A Conservatory Cultural System*, Philadelphia: Temple University Press.

Koenig, John. (2021), *The Dictionary of Obscure Sorrows*, New York: Simon and Schuster.

Kornhaber, Spencer. (2020), "Fiona Apple's Survival Guide to Isolation," *The Atlantic*, April 17. Available online: https://www.theatlantic.com/culture/archive/2020/04/fiona-apple-fetch-bolt-cutters-review/610051/ (accessed August 31, 2022).

Kraugerud, Emil. (2017), "Meanings of Spatial Formation in Recorded Sound," *Journal on the Art of Record Production*, 11.

Krueger, Joel W. (2011), "Doing Things with Music," *Phenomenology and the Cognitive Sciences*, 10 (1): 1–2.

Krueger, Joel W. (2014), "Affordances and the Musically Extended Mind," *Frontiers in Psychology*, 4 (1003): 1–13.

Kurtin, Kate Szer, Nina O'Brien, Deya Roy, and Linda Dam. (2018), "The Development of Parasocial Relationships on YouTube," *Journal of Social Media in Society*, 7 (1): 233–52.

Kurtin, Kate Szer, Nina O'Brien, Deya Roy, and Linda Dam. (2019), "Parasocial Relationships with Musicians," *Journal of Social Media in Society*, 8 (2): 30–50.

Ladano, Mike. (2013), "Review: Johnny Cash-American VI Ain't No Grave." Available online: https://mikeladano.com/2013/08/31/review-johnny-cash-american-vi-aint-no-grave-2010/ (accessed August 31, 2022).

Laurier, C., Olivier Lartillot, Tuomas Eerola, and Petri Toiviainen. (2009), "Exploring Relationships between Audio Features and Emotion in Music," in *Proceedings of the 7th triennial Conference of European Society for the Cognitive Sciences of Music*, 260–4, Jyväskylä, Finland: ESCOM (European Society for the Cognitive Sciences of Music).

Lee, Jung Eun and Brandi Watkins. (2016), "'YouTube Vloggers' Influence on Consumer Luxury Brand Perceptions and Intentions," *Journal of Business Research*, 69 (12): 5753–60.

Leising, Gary. (2018), "Reading 'Racing' as Literature: One Song Seen through an Official Archive as Key to an Album," paper presented at Darkness on the Edge of Town: An International Symposium, West Long Branch, NJ.

Leng, Simon. (2003), *The Music of George Harrison: While My Guitar Gently Weeps*, London: Firefly Publishing.

Levenger, George and Harold L. Raush. (1977), "Preface," in Levenger and Raush (eds), *Close Relationships: Perspectives on the Meaning of Intimacy*, vii–x, Amherst: University of Massachusetts Press.

Levenson, Edgar A. (1974), "Changing Concept of Intimacy in Psychoanalytic Practice," *Contemporary Psychoanalysis*, 10 (3): 359–69.

Lewisohn, Mark. (1995), [Liner notes], in *Anthology 1*, Hollywood: Capitol Records.

Lewisohn, Mark. (1996a), [Liner notes], in *Anthology 2*, Hollywood: Capitol Records.

Lewisohn, Mark. (1996b), [Liner notes], in *Anthology 3*, Hollywood: Capitol Records.

Lewisohn, Mark. (2004), *The Complete Beatles Recording Sessions: The Official Story of the Abbey Road Years 1962–1970*, 3rd edn, London: Hamlyn.

Library of Congress, National Recording Preservation Board. (n.d.), "Recording Registry," Available online: https://www.loc.gov/programs/national-recording-preservation-board/recording-registry/ (accessed August 24, 2022).

Lieck, Ken. (1999), "Genius of Love," *The Austin Chronicle*, March 19. Available online: https://www.austinchronicle.com/music/1999-03-19/521590/ (accessed August 31, 2022).

Lockhart, Paula. (2003), "A History of Early Microphone Singing, 1925–1939: American Mainstream Popular Singing at the Advent of Electronic Microphone Amplification," *Popular Music and Society*, 26 (3): 367–85.

Loviglio, Jason. (2005), *Radio's Intimate Public: Network Broadcasting and Mass-Mediated Democracy*, Minneapolis: University of Minnesota Press.

Lowney, John (2015), "'A New Kind of Music': Jazz Improvisation and the Diasporic Dissonance of Paule Marshall's The Fisher King," *MELUS: Multi-Ethnic Literature of the United States*, 40 (1): 99–123.

Lubell, Gabriel. (2020), "Progressions of Urgency within and across *the White Album*," *Interdisciplinary Literary Studies*, 22 (1–2): 97–117.

Ludwig, William F. II. (2001), *The Making of a Drum Company: The Autobiography of William F. Ludwig II*. Alma: Rebeats Publications.

"Lukas Nelson and Family – 'Just Outside of Austin'", [video], Lukas Nelson, April 27, 2020. Available online: https://youtu.be/uKRW4ioy1ns (accessed August 24, 2022).

MacDonald, Ian. (1994), *Revolution in the Head: The Beatles' Records and the Sixties*, New York: Henry Holt and Company.

Margulis, Elizabeth Hellmuth. (2019), *The Psychology of Music: A Very Short Introduction*, New York: Oxford University Press.

Marsh, Dave. (2004), *Louie Louie*, Ann Arbor: University of Michigan Press.

Marshall, Lee. (2003), "For and against the Record Industry: An Introduction to Bootleg Collectors and Tape Traders," *Popular Music*, 22 (1): 57–72.

Marshall, P. David. (2016), *The Celebrity Persona Pandemic*, Minneapolis: University of Minnesota Press.

Marvin, Carolyn. (1990), *When Old Technologies Were New: Thinking about Electric Communication in the Late Nineteenth Century*, Oxford: Oxford University Press.

Masciotra, David. (2010), *Working on a Dream: The Progressive Political Vision of Bruce Springsteen*, New York: Continuum.

Matthews, Glenna. (1993), "Review of Gender on the Line: Women, the Telephone, and Community Life by Lana F. Rakow," *The Journal of American History*, 80 (2): 756–7.

McAuliffe, Sam. (2021), "Defending the 'Improvisation as Conversation' Model of Improvised Musical Performance," *Jazz Perspectives*, 13 (1): 39–51.

McCracken, Allison. (1999), "'God's Gift to Us Girls': Crooning, Gender, and the Re-Creation of American Popular Song, 1928–1933," *American Music*, 17 (4): 365–95.

McCracken, Allison. (2015), *Real Men Don't Sing: Crooning in American Culture*, Durham, NC: Duke University Press.

McLane, Maureen. (2000), "Critical Response," in Lauren Berlant (ed), *Intimacy*, 435–42, Chicago: University of Chicago Press.

McLeod, Kembrew. (2001), "Genres, Subgenres, Sub-subgenres and More: Musical and Social Differentiation within Electronic/Dance Music Communities," *Journal of Popular Music Studies*, 13 (1): 59–75.

McLuhan, Marshall. ([1962] 1967), *The Gutenberg Galaxy: The Making of Typographic Man*, Toronto: University of Toronto Press.

McLuhan, Marshall and Quentin Fiore. (1968), *War and Peace in the Global Village*, New York: Bantam Books.

McLuhan, Marshall, and Bruce Powers. (1989), *The Global Village: Transformations in World Life and Media in the 21st Century*, New York: Oxford University Press.

Medcalf, Laura Julie. (2016a), "Musical Intimacy and the Negotiation of Boundary Challenges in Contemporary Music Therapy Practice," PhD diss., University of Melbourne, Melbourne.

Medcalf, Laura Julie. (2016b), "Considerations for Therapeutic Boundaries When Using the Intimate Medium of Music," *Voices: A World Forum for Music Therapy*, 16 (2): https://doi.org/10.15845.

Medcalf, Laura Julie and Katrina Skewes McFerran. (2016), "A Critical Interpretive Synthesis of Music Therapy Case Studies: Examining Therapeutic Boundary Themes in the Context of Contemporary Practice," *British Journal of Music Therapy*, 30 (1): 22–35.

Meintjes, Louise. (2003), *Sound of Africa! Making Music Zulu in a South African Studio*, Durham: Duke University Press.

Meyrowitz, Joshua. (1986), "Television and Interpersonal Behavior: Codes of Perception and Response," in Gary Gumpert and Robert Cathcart (eds), *Inter Media: Interpersonal Communication in a Media World*, 3rd edn, 253–72, New York: Oxford University Press.

Middleton, Richard. (1990), *Studying Popular Music*, Milton Keynes: Open University Press.

Miller, Kiri. (2012), *Playing Along: Digital Games, YouTube, and Virtual Performance*, Oxford: Oxford University Press.

Monson, Ingrid. (1996), *Saying Something: Jazz Improvisation and Interaction*, Chicago: University of Chicago Press.

Moore, Allan and Remy Martin. (2019), *Rock: The Primary Text*, 3rd edn, London: Routledge.

Moore, Allan. (2002), "Authenticity as Authentication," *Popular Music*, 21 (2): 209–23.

Morris, Damien. (2018), "Prince: Piano and a Microphone 1983 Review – Intensely Intimate," *The Guardian*, September 23. Available online: https://www.theguardian.com/music/2018/sep/23/prince-piano-and-a-microphone-1983-review (accessed August 31, 2022).

Moylan, William. (2002), *The Art of Recording: Understanding and Crafting the Mix*, 2nd edn, Waltham: Focal Press.

Moylan, William. (2009), "Considering Space in Music," *Journal on the Art of Record Production* (4).

Moylan, William. (2012), "Considering Space in Recorded Music," in Simon Frith and Simon Zagorski-Thomas (eds), *The Art of Record Production: An Introductory Reader for a New Academic Field*, 163–88, Farnham: Ashgate.

Moylan, William. (2015), *Understanding and Crafting the Mix: The Art of Recording*, 3rd edn, Burlington: Focal Press.

"MTV Unplugged," [video] Ibulbu, July 15, 2012. Available online: www.youtube.com/watch?v=GUKpl_sCobQ (accessed August 31, 2022).

"MTV Best of Unplugged Week Commercial 1994," [video] Keith Richardson, August 4, 2016. Available online: www.youtube.com/watch?v=pzlcj6m5qyA (accessed April 33, 2020).

Mulholland, Liam. (2012), "Early Bass Pedals: Speed King and Beyond," *Drum! Magazine*. Available online: http://drummagazine.com/early-bass-pedals-speed-king-beyond/ (accessed August 31, 2022).

National Public Radio. (n.d.), "Tiny Desk," NPR. Available online: https://www.npr.org/series/tiny-desk-concerts/ (accessed August 31, 2022).

Nilsen, Per., Mattheij, jooZt, and Uptown Staff. (2004), *The Vault: The Definitive Guide to the Musical World of Prince*, Linghem: Uptown.

Nowell, Richard. (2012), "Between Dreams and Reality: Genre Personae, Brand Elm Street, and Repackaging the American Teen Slasher Film," *Iluminace*, 24 (3): 69–101.

Oden, Thomas C. (1974), *Game Free: The Meaning of Intimacy*, New York: Dell Publishing.

Oram, Nicholas and Lola Cuddy. (1995), "Responsiveness of Western Adults to Pitch-Distributional Information in Melodic Sequences," *Psychological Research*, 57 (2): 103–18.

Osmond, Humphrey. (1957), "Function as the Basis of Psychiatric Ward Design," *Mental Hospitals*, 8 (4): 23–30.

Patterson, Robert J. (2019), *Destructive Desires: Rhythm and Blues Culture and the Politics of Racial Equality*. New Brunswick: Rutgers University Press.

"Paul Stanley Sings 'Everytime I Look at You' and Talks REVENGE," [video] KISS, March 30, 2020. Available online: https://youtu.be/PWv1x4JC5HI (accessed August 31, 2022).

"Paul Stanley Checks in from Home," KISS, April 6, 2020. Available online: https://youtu.be/_33LCN4zWc4 (accessed August 31, 2022).

Pearce, Susan M. (1995), *On Collecting: An Investigation into Collecting in the European Tradition*. London: Routledge.

Pelly, Jenn. (2020a), "Fiona Apple: Fetch the Bolt Cutters," *Pitchfork*, April 17. Available online: https://pitchfork.com/reviews/albums/fiona-apple-fetch-the-bolt-cutters/ (accessed August 31, 2022).

Pelly, Jenn. (2020b), "Fiona Apple on How She Broke Free and Made the Album of the Year," *Pitchfork*, December 8. Available online: https://pitchfork.com/features/cover-story/fiona-apple-interview/ (accessed August 31, 2022).

Peters, John Durham. (1996), "The Uncanniness of Mass Communication in Interwar Social Thought," *Journal of Communication*, 46 (3): 108–23.

Peters, John Durham. (1999), *Speaking into the Air: A History of the Idea of Communication*, Chicago: University of Chicago Press.

Peters, John Durham. (2004), "The Voice and Modern Media," Originally published in Doris Kolesch and Jenny Schrödl (eds), *Kunst-Stimmen*, Berlin: Theater der Zeit Recherchen. Available online: www.johndurhampeters.com.

Petkovski, Ashley. (2010), "'Walk Like Heroes': The Performed Identity of Bruce Springsteen and the Relationship to Contemporary Popular Music Performance," MA thesis, Ryerson University, Toronto.

Pfeil, Fred. (1993), "Rock Incorporated: Plugging into Axl and Bruce," *Michigan Quarterly Review*, 32 (4): 535–71.

Pinch, Trevor and Karin Bjisterveld. (2004), "Sound Studies: New Technologies and Music," *Social Studies of Science*, 34 (5): 635–48.

du Preez, Amanda and Elaine Lombard. (2014), "The Role of Memes in the Construction of Facebook Personae," *South African Journal for Communication Theory and Research*, 40 (3): 253–70.

Prince. (1982), "How Come U Don't Call Me Anymore" [single], Burbank, CA: Warner Bros. Records.

Prince. (2001), *One Night Alone* [album], Chanhassen, MN: NPG Records.

Prince. (2018), *Piano & a Microphone 1983* [album], Burbank, CA: Warner Bros. Records.

The Promise: The Making of Darkness on the Edge of Town. (2010), [Film] Dir. Thom Zimney, USA: Thrill Hill Productions.

Randall, Linda K. (2011), *Finding Grace in the Concert Hall: Community and Meaning among Springsteen Fans*, Long Grove: Waveland Press.

Randolph, Antonia. (forthcoming), *That's My Heart: Queering Intimacy in Hip-Hop Culture*, Berkeley: University of California Press.

Rapuano, Deborah L. (2001), "Becoming Irish or Becoming Irish Music? Boundary Construction in Irish Music Communities," *Journal of American and Comparative Cultures*, 24 (1–2): 103–13.

Rasmussen, Leslie. (2018), "Parasocial Action in the Digital Age: An Examination of Relationship Building and the Effectiveness of YouTube Celebrities," *Journal of Social Media in Society*, 7 (1): 280–94.

Ratliff, Ben. (2016), *Every Song Ever: Twenty Ways to Listen in an Age of Musical Plenty*, New York: Farrar, Straus and Giroux.

Rauch, Alan. (1988), "Bruce Springsteen and the Dramatic Monologue," *American Studies*, 29 (1): 29–49.

Reddington, Helen. (2018), "Gender Ventriloquism in Studio Production," *IASPM Journal*, 8 (1): 59–73.

Reese, Ashley. (2022), "Why Are Some Zoomers So Wistful for the '80s?," *Jezebel*, January 10. Available online: https://jezebel.com/why-are-some-zoomers-so-wistful-for-the-80s-1848179583 (accessed August 31, 2022).

Reynolds, Simon. (2011), *Retromania: Pop Culture's Addiction to Its Own Past*, New York: Faber and Faber, Inc.

Richman, Joe and Samara Freemark. (2011), "A Nephew's Quest: Who Was Brother Claude Ely?" *All Things Considered* [Radio broadcast]. NPR, May 5. Available online: https://www.npr.org/2011/05/05/136019632/a-nephews-quest-who-was-brother-claude-ely (accessed August 31, 2022).

"Rick Rubin," [podcast episode] *WTF with Marc Maron*, July 19, 2021. Available online: http://www.wtfpod.com/podcast/episode-1245-rick-rubin (accessed August 31, 2022).

Roasting Room. (n.d.), "FAQ." Available online: https://roastingroom.live/faq (accessed August 24, 2022).

Robb-Dover, Kristina. (2012), "Bruce Springsteen as Preacher and Prophet," *Fellowship of Saints and Sinners*. Available online: https://www.beliefnet.com/columnists/fellowshipofsaintsandsinners/2012/03/bruce-springsteen-as-preacher-and-prophet.html (accessed August 31, 2022).

Rollins, Sonny. (1956), "Blue 7" [song], on *Saxophone Colossus*, New York: Blue Note Records.

Rose, Caryn. (2018), "Springsteen on Broadway," *Pitchfork*. Available online: https://pitchfork.com/reviews/albums/bruce-springsteen-springsteen-on-broadway/ (accessed August 31, 2022).

RVG Legacy. (2021), "The Van Gelder Sound: Characteristics." Available online: http://rvglegacy.org/the-van-gelder-sound-characteristics/ (accessed August 31, 2022).

Sawyer, Keith. (2005), "Music and Conversation," in Dorothy Miell, Raymond MacDonald, and David J. Hargreaves (eds), *Musical Communication*, 45–60, Oxford: Oxford University Press.

Scannell, Paddy. (1996), *Radio, Television, and Modern Life*, Cambridge: Blackwell Publishing.

Scannell, Paddy. (2000), "For-Anyone-as-Someone-Structures," *Media, Culture and Society*, 22 (1): 5–24.

Schmidt Horning, Susan. (2004), "Engineering the Performance: Recording Engineers, Tacit Knowledge and the Art of Controlling Sound," *Social Studies of Science*, 34 (5): 703–31.

Schmidt Horning, Susan. (2013), *Chasing Sound: Technology, Culture, and the Art of Studio Recording from Edison to the LP*, Baltimore: Johns Hopkins University Press.

Schuller, Gunther. (1958), "Sonny Rollins and the Challenge of Thematic Improvisation," *Jazz Review*, 1 (1): 6–11.

Scott, Linda M. (1991), "The Troupe: Celebrities as Dramatis Personae in Advertisements," in Rebecca H. Holman and Michael R. Solomon (eds), *Advances in Consumer Research Volume 18*, 355–63, Provo, UT: Association for Consumer Research.

Scott, Suzanne. (2019), *Fake Geek Girls: Fandom, Gender, and the Convergence Culture Industry*, New York: NYU Press.

Seigworth, Gregory J. and Melissa Gregg. (2009), "An Inventory of Shimmers," in Melissa Gregg and Gregory J. Seigworth (eds), *The Affect Theory Reader*, 1–25, Durham: Duke University Press.

Seller, Dermot. (2019), "Authenticity and Its Perceived Significance in Popular Music," Medium, January 16. Available online: https://medium.com/@dermotseller/authenticity-and-its-perceived-significance-in-popular-music-fcf11d3cc5f3 (accessed August 31, 2022).

Sexton, Richard E. and Virginia Staudt Sexton. (1982), "Intimacy: A Historical Perspective," in Martin Fisher and George Stricker (eds), *Intimacy*, 1–20, New York: Plenum Press.

Shank, Barry. (2014), *The Political Force of Musical Beauty*, Durham: Duke University Press.

Shaviro, Steven. (2012), *Without Criteria: Kant, Whitehead, Deleuze, and Aesthetics*, Cambridge: MIT Press.

Sheinbaum, John J. (2010), "'I'll Work for Your Love': Springsteen and the Struggle for Authenticity," in Roxanne Harde and Irwin Streight (eds),

Reading the Boss: Interdisciplinary Approaches to the Works of Bruce Springsteen, 223–42, Lanham: Lexington Books.

Sheinbaum, John J. (2020), "'Movin' Out on Thunder Road: Images of Ambition, Escape, and Authenticity in Billy Joel and Bruce Springsteen," in Ryan Raul Bañagale and John S. Duchan (eds), *We Didn't Start the Fire: Billy Joel and Popular Music Studies*, 29–45, Lanham: Lexington Books.

Sienkiewicz, Matt and Deborah Jaramillo. (2019), "Podcasting, the Intimate Self, and the Public Sphere," *Popular Culture: The International Journal of Media and Culture*, 17 (4): 268–72.

Skea, Dan. (2001), "Rudy Van Gelder in Hackensack: Defining the Jazz Sound in the 1950s," *Current Musicology* (71–73): 54–76.

Small, Christopher. (1998), *Musicking: The Meanings of Performing and Listening*, Middletown: Wesleyan University Press.

Smith, Daniel. (2014), "Charlie is So 'English'-Like: Nationality and the Branded Celebrity Persona in the Age of YouTube," *Celebrity Studies*, 5 (3): 256–74.

Smith, Justin. (2010), *Withnail and Us: Cult Films and Film Cults in British Cinema*, London: I.B. Tauris and Co.

Smith, Stacy L., Katherine Piper, Marc Choueiti, Karla Hernandez, and Kevin Yao. (2021), "Inclusion in the Recording Studio? Gender and Race/Ethnicity of Artists, Songwriters, and Producers across 900 Popular Songs from 2012–2020," USC Annenberg Inclusion Initiative. Available online: http://assets.uscannenberg.org/docs/aii-inclusion-recording-studio2021.pdf (accessed August 31, 2022).

Smith, Thomas. (2019), "Billie Eilish – 'When We All Fall Asleep, Where Do We Go?' Review," *NME*, March 29. Available online: https://www.nme.com/reviews/billie-eilish-album-review-when-we-all-fall-asleep-where-do-we-go-2467653 (accessed August 31, 2022).

Smółka, Maciej. (2021), "The Sound of a City: A Study of the Phenomenon through the Example of the Minneapolis Sound," PhD diss., Jagiellonian University, Krakow.

Snapes, Laura. (2019), "Billie Eilish: When We All Fall Asleep, Where Do We Go? Review – Thrilling Gen Z Terror-Pop," *The Guardian*, March 9. Available online: https://www.theguardian.com/music/2019/mar/29/billie-eilish-when-we-all-fall-asleep-where-do-we-go-review (accessed August 31, 2022).

Sodomsky, Sam. (2020), Elliott Smith. *Pitchfork*, May 24. Available online: https://pitchfork.com/reviews/albums/elliott-smith-elliott-smith/ (accessed August 31, 2022).

Song, Yading, Simon Dixon, Marcus Pearce, and Andrea R. Halpern. (2016), "Perceived and Induced Emotion Responses to Popular Music: Categorical and Dimensional Models," *Music Perception: An Interdisciplinary Journal*, 33 (4): 472–92.

Spinelli, Martin and Lance Dann. (2019), *Podcasting: The Audio Media Revolution*, New York: Bloomsbury.

Stephens, Christopher John. (2018), "'Springsteen on Broadway' Is Springsteen Fully Owning the Myth of the Working Class Hero," *PopMatters*, January 9. Available online: https://www.popmatters.com/springsteen-on-broadway-2623882011.html?rebelltitem=3#rebelltitem3 (accessed August 31, 2022).

Sterne, Jonathan. (2015), "Space within Space: Artificial Reverb and the Detachable Echo," *Grey Room*, 60: 110–31.

Stewart, Susan. (1993), *On Longing: Narratives of the Miniature, the Gigantic, the Souvenir, the Collection*, Durham: Duke University Press.

Stokes, Martin. (2010), *The Republic of Love: Cultural Intimacy in Turkish Popular Music*, Chicago: University of Chicago Press.

Taylor, Timothy D. (1997), *Global Pop: World Musics, World Markets*, London: Routledge.

"TEAC – The History of Sound and Recording," (2022), Tascam Europe, July 25. Available online: https://www.tascam.eu/en/history (accessed 31 August 2022).

"The Rolling Stones Perform You Can't Always Get What You Want | One World: Together at Home," [video] Global Citizen, April 18, 2020. Available online: https://youtu.be/N7pZgQepXfA (accessed August 24, 2022).

Théberge, Paul. (1997), *Any Sound You Can Imagine: Making Music/Consuming Technology*, Hanover: Wesleyan University Press.

Théberge, Paul. (2008), "The End of the World as We Know It: The Changing Role of the Studio in the Age of the Internet," in Simon Frith and Simon Zagorski-Thomas (eds), *The Art of Record Production: An Introductory Reader for a New Academic Field*, 77–90, Farnham: Ashgate.

Thompson, Emily. (2004), *The Soundscape of Modernity: Architectural Acoustics and the Culture of Listening in America, 1900–1933*, Cambridge: MIT Press.

Thompson, Marie and Ian Biddle. (2013), "Introduction: Somewhere between the Signifying and the Sublime," in Marie Thompson and Ian Biddle (eds), *Sound Music Affect: Theorizing Sonic Experience*, 1–43, London: Bloomsbury.

"The Beatles—Anthology I (Press Conference 1995)," [video] Sljhww, June 13, 2018. Available online: youtu.be/w5FSXywuHXY. (accessed August 24, 2022).

Thrift, Nigel. (2005), "But Malice Aforethought: Cities and the Natural History of Hatred," *Transactions of the Institute of British Geographers*, 30 (2): 133–50.

Tillmann, Barbara and Emmanuel Bigand. (1996), "Does Formal Musical Structure Affect Perception of Musical Expressiveness?" *Psychology of Music*, 24 (1): 3–17.

Toppman, Lawrence. (2014), "'Springsteen Rocks Charlotte with Revivalist's flair,'" *Charlotte Observer*. Available online https://www.charlotteobserver.com/entertainment/article9114521.html

Townshend, Pete. (1983), [Liner notes], in *Scoop*, New York: Atco Records.

Turner, Edith. (2012), *Communitas: The Anthropology of Collective Joy*, New York: Palgrave Macmillan.

Turner, Victor. (1969), *The Ritual Process: Structure and Anti-Structure*, New York: Routledge.

Turner, Victor. (1974), *Dramas, Fields, and Metaphors: Symbolic Action in Human Society*, Ithaca: Cornell University Press.

Valentinsson, Mary-Caitlin. (2018), "Stance and the Construction of Authentic Celebrity Persona," *Language in Society*, 47 (5): 715–40.

Velvet Note. (n.d.), "About Us." Available online: https://thevelvetnote.com/about/ (accessed August 24, 2022).

Vento, John. (n.d.), "Steamworks Creative … How It All Started." Available online: https://steamworkscreative.com/about/ (accessed August 24, 2022).

Verbuč, David. (2017), "Notions of Intimate Publicness and the American Do-It-Yourself Music Spaces," *Communication and the Public*, 2 (4): 284–304.

Verbuč, David. (2018), "Theory and Ethnography of Affective Participation at DIY Shows in the US," *Journal of Popular Music Studies*, 30 (1–2): 79–108.

Walhter-Hansen, Mads. (2015), "Sound Events, Spatiality and Diegesis – the Creation of Sonic Narratives in Music Productions," *Danish Musicology Online*. Available online: https://www.danishmusicologyonline.dk/arkiv/arkiv_dmo_uk.html (accessed August 31, 2022).

Ward, Meredith C. (2021), "The Sounds of Lockdown: Virtual Connection, Online Listening, and the Emotional Weight of COVID-19," *Sound Effects: An Interdisciplinary Journal of Sound and Sound Experience*, 10 (1): 8–25.

Watson, Allan, Michael Hoyler, and Christoph Mager. (2009), "Spaces and Networks of Musical Creativity in the City," *Geography Compass*, 3 (2): 856–78.

Waves. (n.d.), "Abbey Road Collection," Waves online. Available online: www.waves.com/bundles/abbey-road-collection#legendary-analog-sound-abbey-road-collection (accessed August 21, 2019)

Waves. (n.d.), "Abbey Road Studio 3," Waves online. Available online: www.waves.com/plugins/abbey-road-studio-3#presenting-the-waves-abbey-road-studio-3-plugin (accessed August 21, 2019).

Wavesfactory. (2021), "SnareBuzz." Available online: https://www.wavesfactory.com/free-audio-plugins/snarebuzz/ (accessed August 31, 2022).

Weinstein, Bruce. (2018), "Lead Like Springsteen: Five Key Things the Boss Does that You Should Too," *Forbes*, June 29, 2022. Available online: https://www.forbes.com/sites/bruceweinstein/2018/06/29/lead-like-springsteen-five-key-things-the-boss-does-that-you-should-too/#11d573081b9a (accessed August 31, 2022).

Weisethaunet, Hans and Ulf Lindberg. (2010), "Authenticity Revisited: The Rock Critic and the Changing Real," *Popular Music and Society*, 33 (4): 465–85.

Welch, Chris and Geoff Nichols. (2001), *John Bonham: A Thunder of Drums*, San Francisco: Backbeat Books.

Whitlock, Bobby. (2011), *A Rock "n" Roll Autobiography*, Jefferson: McFarland and Company.

Wijfes, Huub. (2014), "Spellbinding and Crooning: Sound Amplification, Radio, and Political Rhetoric in International Comparative Perspective, 1900–1945," *Technology and Culture*, 55 (1): 148–85.

Williams, Hayley. (2021), *Flowers for Vases / Descansos [album]*, New York, NY: Atlantic Recordings.

Williams, Raymond. (1965), *The Long Revolution*, Harmondworth: Penguin Books, Ltd.

Wilson, Elizabeth. (2013), *Cultural Passions: Fans, Aesthetes, and Tarot Readers*, London: I.B. Tauris and Co.

Woge, Susan H. (2007), "Songs of the Common Man," *Interdisciplinary Literary Studies*, 9 (1): 139–47.

Wolfe, Paula. (2020), *Women in the Studio: Creativity, Control and Gender in Popular Music Sound Production*, London: Routledge.

Wolff, Bill. (2014), "Springsteen, Tradition, and the Role of the Artist," *BOSS: The Biannual Online-Journal of Springsteen Studies*, 1 (1): 36–73.

Yazdani, Tarss and Don Goede. (2007), *Hi How Are You? The Life, Art, and Music of Daniel Johnston*, San Francisco: Last Gasp.

Zagorski-Thomas, Simon. (2010), "The Stadium in Your Bedroom: Functional Staging, Authenticity and the Audience-Led Aesthetic in Record Production," *Popular Music*, 29 (2): 251–66.

Zagorski-Thomas, Simon. (2018), "Directions in Music by Miles Davis: Using the Ecological Approach to Perception and Embodied Cognition to Analyze the Creative Use of Recording Technology in *Bitches Brew*," *Technology and Culture*, 59 (4): 850–74.

Zelizer, Vivana A. (2007), *The Purchase of Intimacy*, Princeton: Princeton University Press.

Zumthor, Paul. (1990), *Oral Poetry: An Introduction*, trans. Kathy Murphy-Judy, Minneapolis: University of Minnesota Press.

Index

Abbey Road 95–99, 102
affective investment 6–8, 134, 136
"Ain't No Grave" 71–78, 86, 141n7
All Songs Considered 1
American Recordings 72, 77
American VI: Ain't No Grave 72, 75, 78
Anthology (The Beatles) 89–90, 94–104
Apple, Fiona 10, 32, 78–85, 97, 131, 136, 141n11
audiences
    aesthetic 19
    agency 131–32
    and Bruce Springsteen 112–15
    and fandom 7, 89, 91, 103, 107, 136
    and intimacy 4, 89, 106–7, 109–10, 115–16, 121–22, 132, 135–36
    and mass listening 46, 135
    and the musical apparatus 7
    observing 47
    and parasocial relationships 116–18, 122
    and Prince 71
    and relationship with artists 8, 30, 67, 89, 105–7, 109–12, 115–16, 123, 125–26, 128–34
Audio-Technica AT2020 38
authenticity 9, 11, 19, 111–12, 114, 129, 131–34
    "crusade for," 90
    and intimacy 23, 134–36

The Beatles 20, 22–23, 90, 94–104
"Blue 7" 56–65, 86, 141n2
Boilen, Bob 1, 90
Broadway 1

Cash, Johnny 10, 18, 71–78, 141nn7–8
chorus
    and COVID-19 127
    and Dévon Hendryx 36
    and Elliott Smith 34
    and Fiona Apple 79, 81, 83–84
    and Johnny Cash 73–76
    and Prince 68–70, 141n3
    and Sonny Rollins 57–61, 63
    and spatiality 50
    verse-chorus form 49
communication 3, 7, 46, 59
    technology 16, 24, 66–67
communitas 7, 113, 136
Cook-Wilson, Winston 1
Covid-19 pandemic 10, 78, 85, 105, 115, 117–24, 126–28, 139
Crockett, Zachary 1, 90
cultural studies 5, 133, 137
culture 11, 43, 86, 91, 93–96, 106, 135, 137

Dewey, John 11
Digital Audio Workstation 31, 36
digital distribution 27–28, 39, 91, 124, 126–28
digital infrastructure 29, 66, 90
digital mixing 23, 120
digital platforms 3, 16, 110, 117
digital recording 31–33, 51, 127–28
digital spaces 105, 126

Eilish, Billie 9, 32, 37–39, 135

fandom 6–7, 47, 90–92, 131, 136
    fans 1–2, 6–7, 10, 33, 90–92, 95, 98, 100, 102–3, 110–16, 119–20, 128, 131, 134–36
Fensterstock, Alison 1
"Fetch the Bold Cutters" 78–86, 136, 141n11
four-track recorder 30, 134

Grow, Kory 1
The Guardian 1
guitars 21, 34–36, 50, 71, 75–77, 92, 95–96, 114, 120, 123, 126–27, 134

headphones 37–38
Hendryx, Dévon 9, 32, 35–36
home studio 30, 78, 84, 119, 141n11. *See also* recording

intimate space 9, 15, 97, 105–6

Jackson, Michael 103
Johnston, Daniel 3, 9, 32–33
Just a Girl 1

Las Vegas 1
listeners (of music)
   and authenticity 133, 135–36
   and Billie Eilish 37–38
   casual 91, 136
   and Elliott Smith 34
   and engagement 9–10, 24, 33–34, 43, 47–50, 52, 55, 64, 78, 81, 95–100, 107, 132, 136–37
   and fandom 90–92, 136
   and Fiona Apple 81, 86
   groups 6
   and Johnny Cash 74–75, 77
   and musical intimacy 2, 5–6, 8, 10, 20, 26–27, 33–34, 44–47, 49–50, 68, 86, 96, 101–4, 107, 115, 132
   perceptions from 131–32, 137
   and power 27
   and Prince 68–69, 71
   and social bonds 5, 17, 135–36
   solitary 89
   and sonic spaces 22, 24–26, 36, 84–86, 102
   and Sonny Rollins 58–59, 63–64
   and subjectivity 89
   and structure 4
   and transparency 22
listening technologies 38
live performance 94, 110, 114, 116
   and Bruce Springsteen 112
   and *communitas* 136
   and COVID-19 124–25, 127
   and intimacy 2, 10, 105, 120, 136
   and relational labor 115
lyrical aesthetic 73
lyrical content 5, 33–34, 46–49, 51, 59, 74, 76
lyrical expression 64
lyrical narrative 9, 68–71, 78, 80, 82
lyrical relationality 46
lyrical structure 82
lyrics
   and authenticity 136
   and the Beatles 100
   and Bruce Springsteen 112, 114, 134
   and COVID-19 123
   and Dévon Hendryx 35–36
   and Elliott Smith 35
   and Fiona Apple 79–81, 84
   and Johnny Cash 73–74, 77–78
   and musical density 53
   and musical intimacy 9, 43, 46–48, 51, 136
   and Prince 66–71
   and Sonny Rollins 56, 59
   and spontaneous vocalizations 23

mass media 3, 116–17, 124–25
   and affect 7
   audiences 133, 137
   and COVID-19 123
   culture 137
   and fandoms 131
   marketplace 93
   messaging 46
   and nostalgia 93
   and technology 135
media content 6, 117
media ecosystems 16, 93
media personae 117–18, 120
media studies 8, 109, 117–18
media texts 43, 133
microphone 26, 33, 38, 45, 50, 61–62, 64, 66–67, 89, 133
Morris, Damien 1
musical intimacy
   and aesthetic minimalism 96
   and authenticity 11, 132, 134–36
   and The Beatles 94–96, 99–102
   and Billie Eilish 37–38
   and Bruce Springsteen 111
   constructions of 4, 6–9, 15–16, 20, 28, 43, 46, 57, 59–60, 62, 71, 73, 94, 104, 128–29, 134, 137
   definition of 2–3, 5–6

and Dévon Hendryx 35–36
dimensions of 55–56, 62, 65, 85–86
elements of 35, 104
engagement with 106, 129
facilitation of 29, 37, 117
and Fiona Apple 78, 85–86
forms of 31–32, 89–90
and home recording 39
intensity of 136
and Johnny Cash 71–73, 75, 77
and listeners 5–6, 8, 10, 26, 46–47, 68, 86, 96, 101–4, 107, 115
and lyrics 46–48, 68
and nostalgia 10, 92
and parasocial relationships 106, 128
and perception 4, 8, 17, 43, 49, 111, 120, 126, 131, 137
and performance 10, 72, 105, 109, 125, 127–28
and popular music 27–28, 105–6, 131–32, 140n2
promotion of 34
purpose for 33, 104
and Sonny Rollins 56, 63–64
and spatiality 51, 53, 78
and studio recordings 22
and studio space 18–19
and vocal closeness 45–46
musical persona 44, 47, 74, 106, 110–15, 122, 134–35

National Public Radio 1, 89
natural recording environment 38
Netflix 1
New York 18, 20

O'Connell, Finneas 37–39

parasociality 5, 105–6, 110, 116–22, 127–29
Parton, Dolly 103
performance 2, 4, 6, 11, 20, 23, 55–56, 59
conventions of 85, 118, 131–34
co-spatial 22
and COVID 122, 127
and intimacy 48, 105–6, 108, 113–14, 127–28, 131–32, 137
recorded 25–26

resources 30
solo 34, 50, 119–20
sonic 53, 97
space 10, 109–116
venue 9
vocal 35–36, 50, 59, 65–66, 72–74, 76–77, 80, 125–26
persona(e) 9, 44, 91, 99–100, 106, 109–12, 118, 120, 127–28, 132, 134–36
personal lives 2–3
Petty, Tom 103
physical media 15
popular music
   aesthetics of 8–10
   and affect 7–8
   audiences 137
   authenticity 134
   commercial 17
   cultural discourse 2
   and Fiona Apple 82
   forms of 49
   history 21, 98, 133
   industry 31
   and intimacy 2–5, 10–11, 20–21, 43–46, 71, 86, 105, 129, 131–34, 137
   listeners 43
   and lyrics 46–47
   marketplace 90
   and nostalgia 92–93
   and performance 23
   and phone songs 67
   and power dynamics 29
   and Prince 66
   production of 27, 39
   recordings 43, 53, 86, 97–98, 105, 128, 131–32
   and recording studios 15–16, 25
   sonic properties of 8, 55
   technics 17
   and vocal production 79
   Western 82
power dynamics 27–29, 39, 131
Piano and a Microphone 1983 1
Pitchfork 1, 79, 84
Planet Hollywood Resort and Casino 1
Pop Matters 2

Prince 1, 10, 32, 65–71, 98, 131, 141n3, 142n1
proximity effect 34, 38, 52, 64, 67, 73, 105

radio 3, 52, 117
  airplay 96
  broadcasting 8, 15, 43
  and classic rock 94
  shows 115
recording
  aesthetic 33
  and affective quality 69
  archival 6, 103
  and The Beatles 96–99, 101–2
  and Bruce Springsteen 111
  commercial recording studios 15, 17, 22, 27, 39, 70–72, 99, 128
  and consumption 43
  digital 31
  domestic 32, 38, 85
  environment 38, 62, 85
  equipment 19, 29–30, 89
  exhibits 55
  and Fiona Apple 78–85, 136
  four track 134
  home 9–10, 15, 28–30, 34, 38, 49, 78, 85, 90, 97, 99, 123, 132, 135
  home recording aesthetic 29, 31–33, 35–37, 39, 132
  industry 18, 30, 48
  and intimacy 2, 49–51, 55, 66, 73, 86, 99, 111
  and Johnny Cash 71–78
  and latency 125
  and Lizzo 23
  lose-density 50
  and Mark Duffett 92
  media 4, 24
  multimedia 109
  multitrack 34, 50
  and popular music 4, 20–22, 43, 53, 105, 128, 131–32, 137, 142n1
  process 8, 18–20, 26, 31, 45–46, 63–66
  remastered 140n2
  and the Rolling Stones 127
  session 18
  and solos 26, 58–60
  and sonic realism 58

sound 2, 16, 46, 50, 62, 124
space 24–25, 51–52
  and spatiality 52, 95
  storage 1
  studios 9, 15, 17–18, 22, 24, 26–28, 32, 38–39, 51, 80, 128, 136
  and vocal aesthetics 4, 65, 79–80
relational dynamics 6, 15, 58
Rolling Stone 1
Rose, Caryn 1

Smith, Elliot 9, 27, 32, 34, 37, 93, 109, 112
social isolation 10, 85–86, 116, 118, 122–23, 126
social media 98, 110, 116–17, 127–28
social networks 6
soloists 39, 50, 56–60, 71, 118, 125
solo performances 1, 34, 50, 59–61, 65, 95–97, 99, 119
solo recordings 36, 60–64, 99, 102, 134
song construction 9, 43, 48, 53, 60–61, 68–69, 75, 82
song texts 45–46
sonic access 96–99
sonic aesthetic 62
sonic ambience 34, 36
sonic anomalies 20, 25
sonic branding 17
sonic density 23, 84
sonic disorientation 82
sonic environment 29, 50–51
sonic experimentation 18
sonic identity 27
sonic imprint 21
sonic intimacy 35, 72
sonic intrusions 24
sonic markers 16, 98
sonic orientation 122, 126
sonic palette 17, 63, 65, 85, 136
sonic properties 8, 10, 15, 17–20, 32–34, 45–46, 48, 62, 77–80
sonic realism 58
sonic space 22, 24, 34, 50–53, 63–64, 70, 73, 77, 84, 122, 136, 140n2, 141n3
sonic spatiality 9, 36, 50–51, 59, 70, 85
sonic texture 5, 19
sonic uniformity 127
sound media 15

space 8–9, 33–34, 49, 62, 76, 106, 124–26, 128
  acoustic 15–16, 24, 26
  domestic 29, 31, 85, 119, 121
  emotional 68
  gendered 27
  intimate 29, 35–36, 62, 68, 96, 99, 106–7
  performance 10, 119
  physical 16, 24, 36, 49, 62, 70, 118, 121, 128
  recording 25, 32, 35, 84–85
  sonic 22, 24, 34, 50–53, 62–63, 70, 73, 77, 84, 136, 140n2
  studio 17–18, 20, 26, 43, 64, 102
  virtual 116
spatiality 9, 15, 17, 36, 43, 49–53, 59, 62, 69–70, 77, 79–80, 83, 85, 95
Spin 1
Springsteen, Bruce 10, 47, 111–15, 128, 134–35
Stefani, Gwen 1
streaming 1–2, 117
  experience 91–92
  platforms 10, 15, 43, 98, 116
  playlists 135
  space 126
  technology 120
structure (of music) 7–8, 22, 43, 46, 48–49, 59–61, 69, 76–77, 82–84
Swift, Taylor 45, 131, 139

technological innovation 38
Thompson, Ahmir "Questlove" 120
timbre 36, 38, 45–46, 48, 50, 62, 69, 73

verse
  and the Beatles 100
  and Biggie Smalls 52
  and Bruce Springsteen 114
  and Dévon Hendryx 36
  and Elliott Smith 34
  and Fiona Apple 79–80, 82–84
  and Johnny Cash 75–77
  and Paul McCartney 22
  and Prince 68–69
  verse-chorus form 49
vocal address 117–18
vocal aesthetics 4, 21, 23, 34, 36–38, 48, 50–51
vocal closeness 45, 66, 73
vocal comping 76
vocal delivery 23, 35, 45, 66, 69, 74, 79–80
vocal intimacy 67
vocal ontology 44
vocal phrases 20, 22
vocal rhythm 74–75
vocal styles 4, 26, 33–36, 38, 50–51, 59, 65–67, 69–70, 72, 76, 79
vocal tone 47, 80, 85
voice
  and Billie Eilish 37–38
  and corporeality 23
  and distortion 33
  and Fiona Apple 78–79
  and identity 44–46
  and improvisation 58
  and Johnny Cash 71–73, 76–77
  and language 43–45
  and lyrics 59
  male 65–66
  and musical intimacy 9, 43–44, 48
  and naturality 51, 134
  and Prince 66, 69–70
  and Sonny Rollins 56
  and spatiality 70
  and Taylor Swift 45–46
  and tone 116